W9-BRZ-990

Cooking With 5 Ingredients

Appetizers & Beverages
Breads, Brunch & Breakfast
Soups, Salads & Sandwiches
Vegetables & Side Dishes
Main Dishes
Sweets

Recipes with 5 ingredients made in 3 easy steps.

By
Barbara C. Jones

Published By
Cookbook Resources
Highland Village, Texas

Cooking with 5 Ingredients

Additional copies may be obtained
by sending $19.95 plus $4.00 shipping
to address below.

1st Printing   October 2001   20,000 copies

Copyright © 2001
By Cookbook Resources, Highland Village, Texas. All rights reserved.

ISBN 1-931294-10-0

All Rights Reserved. No part of this book may be reproduced in any form without written permission from the publisher, except for brief passages included in a review appearing in a newspaper or magazine with permission from the publisher.

Edited, Designed, Published and Manufactured
in the United States of America
Cookbook Resources, LLC
541 Doubletree Drive
Highland Village, Texas 75418
972/317-0245

Toll Free Orders: 866/229-2665
cookbookresources.com

an imprint of

INTRODUCTION

We are all in a hurry today and Cooking with 5 Ingredients is the "hurry up" way to great meals, easy cooking and the best way to get those compliments from family and friends. Raves are in order when you make the Unbelievable Crab Dip, the Quick Onion Guacamole Dip or the Fiesta Dip. Crabmeat is the wonderful seafood that is just as good canned or fresh. And the Fiesta Dip has a little different twist to the typical Mexican Dip. The Juicy Fruit Dip is spectacular and nectarines are so good. Try it with apples or bananas and you will be feeding the family lots of delicious fruit. Stretch your world to the luscious mango and papaya – eating healthy at the same time. The Tropical Mango Salad is hard to beat!

Whoever heard of spinach sandwiches? They are delicious, creamy and flavorful – perfect for home or afternoon tea. You'll never go wrong on the Butter Mint Salad – it has a fabulous Hawaiian flavor and goes well with any entrée. It is so good you could even use it as a dessert.

Now when your looking for a wonderful chicken dinner for family or friends, the Chicken Marseilles will set your meal apart while taking only a few minutes to "put together". And the Green Bean Revenge will call for a large glass of cold water, but the "hot and spicy" will put your tastebuds in high gear. Mash potatoes are usually family fare, but Creamy Mashed Potatoes will give the potatoes a company taste. And when you are looking for the extra special company flair, try the Chicken Olé or the Carnival Couscous. The couscous has your colorful vegetables and makes a really special dish. For the great ending, the Sunny Lime Pie or the Apricot Cobbler are so quick and easy to make (and good), you'll put it on the menu often.

How many times have you needed to rush foods to the home of a friend in need? The Favorite Cake will be the one you choose – and all the ingredients can be kept on your pantry shelf (except the eggs, but you will have them in the refrigerator). Your **Cooking With 5 Ingredients Cookbook** will give you lots of ideas for "easy fixin" foods to take to that best friend, your church or the party where everybody pitches in.

"Dig In" to the cookbook with great dishes that have only 5 ingredients and give you 3 easy steps to "kitchen fame".

Barbara C. Jones

ABOUT THE AUTHOR

Barbara C. Jones has written 8 cookbooks and has sold more than 400,000 copies. All her cookbooks focus on family dishes that you can serve everyday or on special occasions.

In *Cooking With 5 Ingredients*, she has created shortened versions of many of her favorites and created new combinations that are prepared in 3 easy steps.

Mrs. Jones live in Bonham, Texas. She stays extremely busy with volunteer work, her daughter's publishing business, playing bridge, and cooking for family, friends, and charitable events.

Table of Contents

Notes

APPETIZERS
&
BEVERAGES

Hurrah for Shrimp

1 (8 ounce) package cream cheese, softened
½ cup mayonnaise
1 (6 ounce) can tiny, cooked shrimp, drained
1 ¼ teaspoon Creole (or Cajun) seasoning
1 tablespoon lemon juice

1. Blend cream cheese and mayonnaise in mixer, until creamy.
2. Add shrimp, seasoning and lemon juice; whip only until well mixed.
3. Serve with chips.

   The Creole (or Cajun) seasoning is the key to this great dip!

Favorite Stand-By Shrimp Dip

2 cups cooked, deveined shrimp, finely chopped
2 tablespoons horseradish
½ cup chili sauce
¾ cup mayonnaise
1 tablespoon lemon juice

1. Combine all ingredients with a few sprinkles of salt and refrigerate. (If shrimp has been frozen, be sure to drain well.
2. Serve with cucumber or zucchini slices.

Fiesta Dip

1 (15 ounce) can tamales
1 (16 ounce) can chili without beans
1 cup picante sauce
2 (5 ounce) jars Old English cheese
1 cup finely chopped onion

1. Mash tamales with a fork.
2. In saucepan, combine all ingredients; heating to mix.
3. Serve hot with crackers or chips.

Unbelievable Crab Dip

1 (16 ounce) box Velveeta cheese
2 (6.5 ounce) cans crabmeat, drained
1 bunch fresh green onions, chopped, tops too
2 cups mayonnaise
½ teaspoon seasoned salt

1. Melt cheese in top of double boiler. Add remaining ingredients.
2. Serve hot (or room temperature) with Wheat Thins or Wheatables. Absolutely delicious!

Don't count on your guest leaving the dip table
until this dip is gone!

Jump In Crab Dip

1 (6 ounce) can white crabmeat
1 (8 ounce) package cream cheese
1 stick butter (the real thing)

1. In a saucepan, combine crabmeat, cream cheese and butter. Heat and mix thoroughly.
2. Transfer to hot chafing dish. Serve with chips.

This is so good you will wish you had doubled the recipe!

Crab Dip Kick

1 (8 ounce) package cream cheese, softened
3 tablespoons picante sauce
2 tablespoons prepared horseradish
1 (6 ounce) can crabmeat, drained and flaked

1. In mixing bowl, beat cream cheese until creamy; add the picante and horseradish; mixing well.
2. Stir in the crabmeat. Refrigerate.
3. Serve with assorted crackers.

Hot Broccoli Dip

1 (16 ounce) box Mexican Velveeta cheese
1 (10 ounce) can golden mushroom soup
1 (10 ounce) box frozen chopped broccoli, thawed

1. In saucepan over medium heat, combine cheese and soup. Stir constantly until cheese is melted.
2. Stir broccoli into cheese-soup mixture.
3. Serve hot with chips.

Zippy Broccoli Cheese Dip

1 (10 ounce) package frozen chopped broccoli, thawed and drained
2 tablespoons margarine
2 ribs celery, chopped
1 small onion, finely chopped
1 (1 pound) box mild Mexican Velveeta cheese, cubed

1. Make sure broccoli is thoroughly thawed and drained. Place margarine in a large saucepan and saute the broccoli, celery and onion at medium heat for about 5 minutes, stirring several times.
2. Add cheese and heat, stirring constantly, just until cheese is melted.
3. Serve hot with chips.

If you want the "zip" to be zippier, use hot Mexican Velveeta cheese instead of the mild.

Spicy Beef and Cheese Dip

1 (10 ounce) can Rotel tomatoes and green chilies
½ teaspoon garlic powder
1 (2 pound) box Velveeta cheese
1 pound lean ground beef, browned and cooked

1. In a large saucepan, place tomatoes and green chilies, garlic and cheese cut in chunks. (Use Mild Mexican Velveeta if you like it really spicy.) Heat on low until cheese is melted.
2. Add the ground beef, mixing well.
3. Serve with tortilla chips.

Hot Sombrero Dip

2 (15 ounce) cans bean dip
1 pound lean ground beef, browned and cooked
1 (4 ounce) can green chilies
1 cup hot picante sauce
1 ½ cups shredded cheddar cheese

1. Layer bean dip, ground beef, chilies and picante sauce in a 3 quart baking dish. Top with cheese.
2. Bake at 350 degrees just until cheese is melted, about 10 or 15 minutes.
3. Serve with tortilla chips.

Spinach Cheese Dip

1 (10 ounce) package frozen chopped spinach, thawed
2 (8 ounce) packages cream cheese, softened
1 (1.2 ounce) package Knorr vegetable soup mix, dry
1 (8 ounce) can water chestnuts, chopped

1. Drain spinach on several paper towels. Squeeze or mash spinach into towels several times to make sure all water is gone from the spinach.
2. In mixer bowl, beat the cream cheese until smooth. Fold in the spinach, soup mix and water chestnuts. Chill.
3. Serve with chips or crackers.

I have listed 3 dips that are basically spinach dips. All three (Spinach Cheese Dip, Vegetable Dip and Green Wonder Dip) are a little different – creamy, crunchy or spicy, they are all great. Even spinach haters will like these dips.

Veggie Dip

1 (10 ounce) package frozen chopped spinach, thawed and WELL drained
1 bunch chopped fresh green onions, chopped, tops too
1 (.9 ounce) envelop Lipton vegetable soup mix (dry)
1 tablespoon lemon juice
2 (8 ounce) cartons sour cream

1. Drain spinach on several paper towels.
2. In a medium bowl, combine all ingredients adding a little salt. (Adding several drops of Tabasco is also good.) Cover and refrigerate.
3. Serve with chips.

   You will have the family saying "You mean this is spinach!"

Green Wonder Dip

1 (10 ounce) package frozen, chopped spinach, thawed
1 (1 ⅝ once) package Knorr Swiss vegetable soup mix (dry)
½ cup minced onion
1 cup mayonnaise
1 cup sour cream

1. Drain spinach well by pressing out all excess water. (Using paper towels is the best way to get all excess water out of spinach).
2. Combine all ingredients and mix well. Cover and refrigerate overnight.
3. Serve with crackers, chips or raw vegetable sticks.

The Big Dipper

1 (15 ounce) can chili (no beans)
1 (10 ounce) can Ro-Tel tomatoes and green chilies
1 (16 ounce) box Velveeta cheese, cubed
½ cup chopped green onions
½ teaspoon cayenne pepper

1. In saucepan, combine all ingredients. Heat just until cheese melts, stirring constantly.
2. Serve warm with assorted dippers or toasted French bread sticks.

Sassy Onion Dip

1 (8 ounce) package cream cheese, softened
1 (8 ounce) carton sour cream
½ cup chili sauce
1 package dry onion soup mix
1 tablespoon lemon juice

1. In mixer bowl, beat cream cheese until fluffy. Add remaining ingredients and mix well.
2. Cover and chill. Serve with strips of raw zucchini, celery, carrots, etc.

Plain and simple, but great!

Pizza In A Bowl

1 pound lean ground beef
1 (26 ounce) jar marinara or spaghetti sauce
2 teaspoons dried oregano
1 (16 ounce) package shredded mozzarella cheese
¾ teaspoon garlic powder

1. In a saucepan, cook beef over medium heat until no longer pink; drain.
2. Stir in marinara sauce and oregano; simmer about 15 minutes. Gradually stir in cheese until melted.
3. Pour into a fondue pot or small slow cooker to keep warm. Serve with Italian toast (Panetini – found in the deli.)

Monterey Jack's Dip

1 (8 ounce) package cream cheese, softened and whipped
1 (16 ounce) can chili (no beans)
1 (4 ounce) can diced green chilies
1 (8 ounce) package grated Monterey jack cheese
1 (4 ounce) can chopped black olives

1. Using a 7 x 11 inch glass baking dish, layer the ingredients in the order given.
2. Bake uncovered at 325 degrees for 30 minutes.
3. Serve with chips.

Hot Corn Dip

1 (15 ounce) can whole kernel corn, drained
1 (7 ounce) can chopped green chilies, drained
½ cup chopped sweet red pepper
1 ½ cups shredded colby and monterey jack cheese
¼ cup mayonnaise

1. In a bowl, combine the corn, chilies, red pepper and cheeses. Stir in mayonnaise. (Adding ½ cup chopped walnuts makes this dip even better.)
2. Transfer to an ungreased 2 quart baking dish.
3. Cover and bake at 325 degrees for 35 minutes. Serve hot with tortilla chips.

Sometimes the green chilies are not very hot so I like to add a pinch or two of red pepper.

Quick Mix Dip

1 (8 ounce) package cream cheese, softened
1 cup mayonnaise
1 (1 ounce) package Hidden Valley Ranch salad dressing mix
½ onion, finely minced

1. In mixer bowl, combine cream cheese and mayonnaise and beat until creamy.
2. Stir in salad dressing mix and onion.
3. Chill and serve with fresh vegetables.

Ham It Up

2 (8 ounce) packages cream cheese, softened
2 (6 ounce) cans deviled ham
2 heaping tablespoons horseradish
¼ cup minced onion
¼ cup finely chopped celery

1. In mixer, beat cream cheese until creamy.
2. Add all other ingredients
3. Chill and serve with crackers. (This would also make little party sandwiches, using the party rye bread.)

Ham It Up Some More Dip

1 (16 ounce) carton small curd cottage cheese
2 (6 ounce) cans deviled ham
1 package onion soup mix, dry
½ cup sour cream
2 tablespoons lemon juice

1. Blend cottage cheese in blender or mixer.
2. Add ham, soup mix, sour cream and lemon juice mixing well.
3. Serve with crackers.

I like to add a little "zip" in this dip by adding several dashes of Tabasco.

Creamy Dilly Dip

1 (8 ounce) carton sour cream
1 cup mayonnaise, 2 tablespoon lemon juice
4 chopped green onions, tops too
1 tablespoon dill weed
2 teaspoons White Wine Worcestershire sauce

1. Combine all ingredients until well blended. (Do not use the darker Worcestershire – the White Wine Worcestershire keeps this dip light in color and texture.)
2. Sprinkle lightly with paprika for color. Cover and refrigerate.
3. Serve with carrot sticks, broccoli flowerets or jicama sticks.

Curry Lover's Veggie Dip

1 cup mayonnaise
½ cup sour cream
1 teaspoon curry powder
¼ teaspoon Tabasco
1 teaspoon lemon juice

1. Combine all ingredients and mix until well blended.
2. Sprinkle a little paprika for color. Cover and refrigerate. Serve with raw vegetables.

Roquefort Dip

1 (8 ounce) package cream cheese, softened
2 cups mayonnaise
1 small onion, finely grated
1 (3 ounce) package Roquefort cheese, crumbled
⅛ teaspoon garlic powder

1. In mixer bowl, combine cream cheese and mayonnaise. Beat until creamy.
2. Add onion, Roquefort cheese and garlic powder, mixing well. Refrigerate.
3. Serve with zucchini sticks, turnip sticks or cauliflower flowerets.

Veggie Dive Dip

1 cup mayonnaise
1 (8 ounce) carton sour cream
1 ½ teaspoons Beau Monde seasoning
1 teaspoon dill weed, 2 tablespoons parsley
1 bunch green onions, chopped, tops too

1. Stir all ingredients together and chill. Better if made a day ahead.
2. Serve with celery sticks, broccoli flowerets, jicama sticks or carrot sticks.

La Cucaracha

1 (12 ounce) package chorizo, sliced or cut up
1 (1 pound) box Mexican style Velveeta cheese
1 (15 ounce) can stewed tomatoes

1. Saute chorizo until cooked; drain.
2. In double boiler, on medium heat, melt cheese and tomatoes, stirring constantly.
3. Combine chorizo, cheese and tomatoes; mixing well. Serve with tortilla chips.

California Clam Dip

1 envelope onion soup mix (dry)
2 (8 ounce) cartons sour cream
1 (7 ounce) can minced clams, drained
3 tablespoons chili sauce
1 tablespoon lemon juice

1. Combine onion soup mix and sour cream; mixing well.
2. Add clams, chili sauce and lemon juice.
3. Chill. Serve with assorted crackers.

Zesty Clam Dip

1 (15 ounce) can New England clam chowder
1 (8 ounce) and 1 (3 ounce) package cream
  cheese, softened
2 tablespoons minced onion
2 tablespoons prepared horseradish
2 tablespoons white wine Worcestershire

1. Combine all ingredients and blend in food processor; process until smooth.
2. Serve with raw vegetables or chips.

Roasted Garlic Dip

4 or 5 unpeeled whole garlic cloves
2 (8 ounce) packages cream cheese, softened
¾ cup mayonnaise
1 (7 or 9 ounce) jar sweet roasted red peppers,
  drained, coarsely chopped
1 bunch fresh green onions, chopped (tops too)

1. Preheat oven to 400 degrees. Lightly brush outside of garlic bulbs with a little oil and place in shallow baking pan. Heat about 10 minutes. Cool. Press roasted garlic out of cloves.
2. Beat together cream cheese and mayonnaise until creamy. Add remaining ingredients; mixing well. The roasted peppers are great in this recipe, but if you want it a little spicy, add several drops of Tabasco.
3. Sprinkle with red pepper or paprika and serve with chips.

Great Guacamole

4 avocados, peeled
About ½ cup Picante sauce
¼ cup sour cream
1 teaspoon salt

1. Split avocados and remove seeds. Mash avocado with a fork.
2. Add Picante, sour cream and salt.
3. Serve with tortilla chips.

Place one of the avocado seeds in the dip until time to serve – the seed keeps the color bright.

Avocado and Onion Dip

1 package Lipton's golden onion soup mix
1 (8 ounce) carton sour cream
½ cup mayonnaise
2 ripe avocados, mashed
1 tablespoon lemon juice

1. Mix together all ingredients, working quickly so the avocados won't turn dark.
2. Place in container with one of the avocado seeds (that keeps the avocado from turning dark).
3. Serve with Wheat Thins.

Quick Onion Guacamole

1 (8 ounce) carton sour cream
1 package onion soup mix (dry)
2 (8 ounce) cartons avocado dip
2 green onions, chopped, tops too
½ teaspoon crushed dill weed

1. Mix all ingredients together and chill.
2. Serve with chips.

Tasty Tuna

1 (6 ounce) can solid white tuna, drained and
**   flaked**
1 envelope Good Seasons Zesty Italian salad
**   dressing mix, dry**
1 tablespoon lemon juice
1 (8 ounce) carton sour cream
3 green onions, chopped (tops too)

1. Combine all ingredients, stirring until blended. Chill.
2. Serve with melba rounds.

Cucumber Dip

2 medium cucumbers
2 (8 ounce) packages cream cheese, softened
Several drops Tabasco
1 package Hidden Valley Ranch dressing mix
½ teaspoon garlic powder

1. Peel cucumbers, cut in half lengthwise and scoop out seeds. Chop cucumbers in very fine pieces (or in a food processor). In mixer, combine cream cheese, Tabasco, dressing mix and garlic powder; beat until creamy.
2. Combine cucumbers and cream cheese mixture, mixing well. (½ cup chopped pecans makes this dip even better.) Serve with chips.

This dip makes great "party" sandwiches made with thin
sliced white bread. If you do use it for sandwiches, make
sure you squeeze all the water out of the cucumbers.

Poor Man's Pate

1 (16 ounce) roll Braunscweiger, room
**   temperature**
1 package onion soup mix
1 (8 ounce) carton sour cream
1 (8 ounce) package cream cheese, softened
Several dashes Tabasco

1. Mash Braunschweiger (goose liver) with fork.
2. With the mixer, beat the remaining ingredients together until fairly creamy.
3. Add the Braunschweiger, mixing well. Refrigerate. Serve with chips.

Sweet Onions

**5 sweet onions, chopped
(Vidalia onions if available)
1 cup sugar
½ cup white vinegar
⅔ cup mayonnaise
1 teaspoon celery salt**

1. Soak onions in the sugar, vinegar and 2 cups water for about 3 hours. Drain.
2. Toss with mayonnaise and celery salt.
3. Serve on crackers.

Cheese Strips

**1 loaf thin-sliced bread
1 (8 ounce) package shredded cheddar cheese
6 slices bacon, fried, drained and coarsely broken
½ cup chopped onion
1 cup mayonnaise**

1. Remove crust from bread. Combine next 4 ingredients and spread filling over slices; cut into 3 strips. Place on cookie sheet.
2. Bake at 400 degrees for 10 minutes.
3. For a special touch, add ⅓ cup slivered almonds, toasted.

Blue Cheese Crisps

2 (4 ounce) packages crumbled blue cheese
1 stick margarine, softened
1 ⅓ cups flour
⅓ cup poppy seeds
¼ teaspoon ground red pepper

1. Beat blue cheese and margarine at medium speed until fluffy. Add flour, poppy seed and red pepper; beat until blended.
2. Divide dough in half; shape each portion into a 9 inch log. Cover and refrigerate 2 hours.
3. Cut each log into ¼ inch slices and place on ungreased baking sheet. Bake at 350 degrees for 13 to 15 minutes or until golden grown. Cool.

Party Smokies

1 cup catsup
1 cup plum jelly
1 tablespoon lemon juice
4 tablespoons prepared mustard
2 (5 ounce) packages tiny smoked sausages

1. In a saucepan, combine all ingredients except sausages and heat; mix well.
2. Add sausages and simmer for 10 minutes.
3. Serve hot with cocktail toothpicks.

Sausage and Pineapple Bits

1 pound link (cooked) sausage, skinned
1 pound hot bulk sausage
1 (15 ounce) can crushed pineapple, undrained
2 cups packed brown sugar
1 tablespoon White Wine Worcestershire

1. Slice link sausage into ⅓ inch pieces. Shape bulk sausage into one inch balls. In a skillet, brown sausage balls.
2. In a large saucepan, combine pineapple, brown sugar and white Worcestershire
3. Heat and add both sausages. Simmer for 30 minutes. Serve in chafing dish or a small crock pot with cocktail picks.

The "sweet and hot" make a delicious combo.

Sausage Balls

2 cups Bisquick mix
1 pound hot sausage
1 cup shredded cheddar cheese

1. Mix the Bisquick, sausage and cheese with a wooden spoon – or you might want to mix with your hands.
2. Shape into 1 inch balls; place on a cookie sheet and bake at 350 degrees for about 20 minutes. These will freeze nicely.

Raspberry Glazed Wings

¾ cup seedless raspberry jam
¼ cup cider vinegar
¼ cup soy sauce
1 teaspoon garlic powder
16 whole chicken wings (about 3 pounds)

1. In saucepan, combine jam, vinegar, soy sauce, garlic and 1 teaspoon black pepper. Bring to a boil; boil 1 minute.
2. Cut chicken wings into three sections; discard wing tips. Place wings in a large bowl; add raspberry mixture and toss to coat. Cover and refrigerate for 4 hours.
3. Line a 10 x 15 inch baking pan with foil and grease the foil. Using a slotted spoon and reserving the marinade, place wings in pan.
4. Bake uncovered at 350 degrees for 30 minutes, turning once. Cook reserved marinade for 10 minutes; brush over wings and bake 25 minutes longer.

Curried Wings

10 chicken wings
¼ cup margarine, melted
¼ cup honey
¼ cup prepared mustard
1 ¼ teaspoon curry powder

1. Cut off wingtips and discard. Cut wings in half at joint.
2. Combine next 4 ingredients in a large zip-top plastic bag. Add chicken and seal. Refrigerate at least 2 hours, turning chicken occasionally.
3. Remove chicken from marinade, discarding marinade. Place chicken in a greased 9 x 13 inch baking dish. Bake uncovered at 325 degrees for 1 hour.

Cocktail Ham Roll-Ups

1 (3 ounce) package cream cheese, softened
1 teaspoon finely grated onion
Mayonnaise
1 (3 ounce) package sliced ham
1 (15 ounce) can asparagus spears

1. Combine cream cheese, grated onion and enough mayonnaise to make spreading consistency.
2. Separate sliced ham, spread mixture on slices and place an asparagus spear (or two) on ham and roll. Cut each roll into 4 pieces.
3. Spear each piece with a toothpick for serving. Refrigerate.

This can also be used when serving a salad luncheon –
perhaps serving these Ham Roll-Ups (not cutting into
pieces), the Broccoli-Cauliflower Salad
and the Tropical Mango Salad.

Cheese Straws

1 (5 ounce) package pie crust mix
¾ cup shredded cheddar cheese
Cayenne pepper

1. Prepare pie crust according to package directions. Roll out into a rectangular shape. Sprinkle cheese over dough. Press the cheese into the dough. Sprinkle cayenne pepper over the cheese. Fold dough over once to cover cheese.
2. Roll out to make a ¼ inch thickness. Cut dough into ½ by 3 inch strips and place on a lightly greased cookie sheet.
3. Bake at 350 degrees for 12 to 15 minutes or until lightly brown.

Green Eyes

4 medium size dill pickles
4 slices boiled ham
Light cream cheese, softened
Black pepper

1. Dry off pickles. Lightly coat one side of the ham slices with cream cheese and sprinkle on a little pepper. Roll the pickle up in the ham slice coated with cream cheese.
2. Chill. Slice into circles to serve.

Here's lookin' at ya!

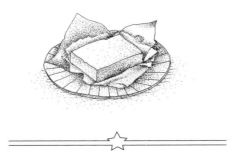

Kids' Dogs

1 package of 10 wieners
3 cans biscuits (with 10 biscuits per can)
Dijon mustard

1. Cut each wiener in thirds. Take each biscuit and flatten slightly and spread with mustard.
2. Wrap each wiener piece in a biscuit; pinch to seal.
3. Bake at 400 degrees for 10 to 12 minutes or until lightly brown.

A kid's favorite!

Chestnuts Under Wraps

1 (8 ounce) can whole water chestnuts, drained
¼ cup soy sauce
About ½ pound bacon, cut in thirds

1. Marinate water chestnuts for an hour in soy sauce. Wrap ⅓ slice bacon around the water chestnuts and fasten with a tooth pick.
2. Bake at 375 degrees for 20 minutes or until bacon is done. Drain and serve hot.

Mini Reubens

½ cup Thousand Island dressing
24 slices party rye bread
1 ⅓ cups well-drained chopped sauerkraut
½ pound thinly sliced corned beef
¼ pound sliced Swiss cheese

1. Spread dressing on slices of bread. Place 1 slice corned beef on bread; top with sauerkraut.
2. Cut cheese the size of bread and place over sauerkraut.
3. Place open-face sandwiches on cookie sheet. Bake at 375 degrees for 10 minutes or until cheese melts.

Chicken Lickers

2 white onions, sliced
10 to 12 chicken livers
4 strips bacon
⅓ cup sherry

1. Place onion slices in shallow pan. Top each onion slice with a chicken liver and ⅓ strip bacon. Pour sherry over all.
2. Bake, uncovered at 350 degrees for about 45 minutes or until bacon is crisp. Baste occasionally with pan drippings.

Oyster Bites Bacon

1 (5 ounce) can smoked oysters, drained and
**   chopped**
⅔ cup herb-seasoned stuffing mix, crushed
¼ cup water
8 slices bacon, halved and partially cooked

1. Combine oysters, stuffing mix and water. Add another teaspoon water if mixture seems too dry. Form into balls, using about 1 tablespoon mixture for each.
2. Wrap a half slice of bacon around each and secure with a toothpick. Place on a rack in a shallow baking pan.
3. Cook at 350 degrees for 25 to 30 minutes or until bacon is crisp.

Drunk Franks

1 package wieners
½ cup chili sauce
½ cup packed brown sugar
½ cup bourbon

1. Cut wieners into bite-size pieces. Combine chili sauce, sugar and bourbon in a saucepan. Add wieners to sauce and simmer 30 minutes.
2. Serve in chafing dish.

Cheddar Puffs

1 stick margarine, softened
1 cup grated cheddar cheese
1 ¼ cups flour
¼ teaspoon salt

1. Blend together the margarine and cheese until fairly smooth. Stir in flour and salt. Knead lightly with hands. Roll, a teaspoon at a time, into balls.
2. Place on cookie sheet.
3. Bake at 375 degrees for 14 to 15 minutes or until golden. Serve hot.

No-Fuss Meatballs

1 (14 ounce) package frozen cooked meatballs, thawed
1 tablespoon soy sauce
½ cup chili sauce
⅔ cup grape jelly (or plum jelly)
¼ cup Dijon mustard

1. In a skillet, cook meatballs in soy sauce until heated through.
2. Combine the chili sauce, jelly and mustard; pour over the meatballs. Cook and stir until jelly is dissolved and mixture comes to a boil.
3. Reduce heat; cover and simmer for about 5 minutes.

Sausage Rounds

1 (8 ounce) package crescent dinner rolls
1 pound sausage, uncooked

1. Open package of rolls and smooth out dough with a rolling pin, sealing the seams.
2. Break up sausage with hands and spread a thin layer of sausage over rolls. Roll into a log. Wrap in wax paper and freeze several hours.
3. Slice into ¼ inch rounds. Place on cookie sheet and bake at 350 degrees for 20 minutes or until lightly browned.

The Queen's Cheese Ball

1 stick margarine, softened
1 (6 ounce) jar Old English cheese, softened
1 cup plus 2 tablespoons flour
¼ teaspoon cayenne pepper
½ teaspoon salt

1. In a bowl, mix all ingredients together, working in flour gradually.
2. Form into marble sized balls and flatten with fork.
3. Bake at 400 degrees for 6 to 8 minutes or until lightly brown.

Olive Cheese Balls

2 ¼ cups shredded sharp cheddar cheese
1 cup flour
1 stick margarine, melted
1 (5 ounce) jar green olives

1. In large bowl, combine the cheese and flour. Add the margarine and mix well.
2. Cover olives with mixture and form balls.
3. Bake at 350 degrees for about 15 minutes or until lightly brown.

Caviar Delights Artichoke

2 (8 ounce) packages cream cheese, softened
1 (14 ounce) can artichoke hearts, drained and
**   chopped**
½ cup finely grated onion
1 (3 ounce) jar caviar, drained
3 hard-boiled eggs, grated

1. Beat cream cheese until smooth; add artichoke hearts and onion.
2. Spread in an 8 or 9 inch glass pie plate. Chill.
3. Before serving, spread caviar on top of cream cheese mixture and place grated egg on top. Serve with crackers.

Hot Artichoke Spread

1 (14 ounce) can artichoke hearts, drained, finely
**   chopped**
1 (4 ounce) can chopped green chilies
1 cup mayonnaise
1 (8 ounce) package shredded mozzarella cheese
½ teaspoon garlic powder

1. Remove any spikes or tough leaves from artichoke hearts.
2. Combine all ingredients, mixing thoroughly. Pour into a 9 inch square baking pan and sprinkle some paprika over top.
3. Bake at 325 degrees for 25 minutes. Serve hot with assorted crackers.

Black Olive Spread

1 (8 ounce) package cream cheese, softened
½ cup mayonnaise
1 (4 ounce) can chopped black olives
3 green onions, chopped very fine

1. Whip together the cream cheese and mayonnaise until smooth. Add olives and onions. Chill.
2. Spread on slices of party rye.

Jiffy Tuna Spread

1 (7 ounce) can white tuna, drained and flaked
½ cup chopped ripe olives
1 package Good Seasons Italian salad dressing mix, dry
1 (8 ounce) carton sour cream

1. Combine all ingredients, mixing well.
2. Sprinkle with a little paprika for color and serve on crackers.

Walnut Cheese Spread

¾ cup walnuts, roasted and chopped
1 (16 ounce) package shredded cheddar cheese
3 green onions, chopped, tops too
½ to ¾ cup mayonnaise
½ teaspoon liquid smoke

1. (To roast walnuts, place in a 250 degree oven for 10 minutes.)
2. Combine all ingredients and let stand in refrigerator overnight.
3. Spread on assorted crackers.

Smoked Oyster Spread

1 (8 ounce) package cream cheese, softened
3 tablespoons mayonnaise
1 (3 ½ ounce) can smoked oysters, chopped
½ teaspoon onion salt
2 tablespoons parmesan cheese

1. Whip cream cheese and mayonnaise until creamy.
2. Add oysters, onion salt and cheese.
3. Mix well and dip or spread on crackers.

Spicy Cheese Round

1 pound hot sausage
1 cup chunky hot Picante sauce
1 pound Velveeta cheese, cut in chunks
1 pound shredded sharp cheddar cheese
1 pound shredded mild cheddar cheese

1. Brown sausage in large roaster. Add Picante sauce (and ½ teaspoon garlic powder if you like).
2. Add Velveeta cheese, turning burner on low. Stir constantly while cheese is melting. Add the Cheddar cheeses while stirring. It will be hard to stir, but you must keep stirring to keep it from burning.
3. Pour into a Pam sprayed bundt pan. Refrigerate overnight. Unmold onto a platter. It would be nice to place parsley around the ring. To serve, cut slices of the cheese mold and serve with Wheatsworth crackers.

This is really a "big" party ring of seasoned cheese.
The shape of the bundt pan makes it elegant
as well as delicious.

Ginger Fruit Dip

1 (3 ounce) package cream cheese, softened
1 (7 ounce) jar marshmallow cream
½ cup mayonnaise
1 teaspoon ground ginger
1 teaspoon grated orange rind

1. Beat cream cheese at medium speed until smooth; add marshmallow cream and next 3 ingredients, stirring until smooth.
2. Serve with fresh fruit sticks.

Kahlua Fruit Dip

1 (8 ounce) package cream cheese, softened
1 (8 ounce) carton Cool Whip
⅔ cup packed brown sugar
⅓ cup Kahlua
1 (8 ounce) carton sour cream

1. With mixer, whip cream cheese until creamy and fold in Cool Whip.
2. Add sugar, Kahlua and sour cream, mixing well.
3. Refrigerate 24 hours before serving with fresh fruit.

Juicy Fruit Dip

1 (8 ounce) package cream cheese, softened
2 (7 ounce) cartons marshmallow cream
½ teaspoon cinnamon
⅛ teaspoon ground ginger

1. With mixer, combine and beat together all ingredients. Mix well.
2. Refrigerate.
3. Serve with unpeeled slices of nectarines or apple slices. Delicious!

Fruit'n Crackers

1 (8 ounce) package cream cheese, softened
2 tablespoons orange juice
1 ½ teaspoons Triple Sec
1 (11 ounce) package Wheatsworth crackers
Several kiwi fruit

1. Beat together the cream cheese, orange juice and Triple Sec. Lightly toast crackers in 350 degree oven for 10 minutes. Spread crackers with cream cheese mixture.
2. Decorate tops of crackers with fruit.

Ginger Cream

1 (8 ounce) package cream cheese, softened
1 stick unsalted margarine, softened
2 tablespoons milk
3 tablespoons finely chopped crystallized ginger

1. Combine all ingredients in mixer. Beat until creamy.
2. Spread on your favorite fruit or nut breads.

Peanut Butter Spread

1 (8 ounce) package cream cheese, softened
1 ⅔ cups creamy peanut butter
½ cup powdered sugar
1 tablespoon milk

1. In mixer, cream together all ingredients.
2. Serve spread with apple wedges or graham crackers.

Ambrosia Spread

1 (11 ounce) can mandarin orange sections, drained
1 (8 ounce) container soft cream cheese with pineapple, softened
¼ cup flaked coconut, toasted
¼ cup slivered almonds, chopped and toasted

1. Chop the orange sections and set aside.
2. Whip the cream cheese and fold in coconut and almonds.
3. Spread on date nut bread, banana bread, etc. To toast coconut and almonds, bake at 325 degrees for 10 minutes.

Orange Cheese Spread

2 (8 ounce) packages cream cheese, softened
⅔ cup powdered sugar
1 tablespoon orange peel, grated
2 tablespoons Grand Marnier
2 tablespoons frozen orange juice concentrate, undiluted

1. Blend all ingredients together in mixer until smooth. Refrigerate.
2. Spread on dessert breads to make sandwiches or this can be used as a dip for fruit.

Green Olive Spread

1 (8 ounce) package cream cheese
⅔ cup mayonnaise
¾ cup chopped pecans
1 cup green olives, drained and chopped
¼ teaspoon black pepper

1. In mixer, blend cream cheese and mayonnaise until smooth.
2. Add remaining ingredients, mixing well; refrigerate.
3. Serve on crackers or make sandwiches with party rye bread.

Beef or Ham Spread

1 pound leftover roast beef or ham
¾ cup sweet pickle relish
½ onion, finely diced
2 celery ribs, chopped
2 hard-boiled eggs, chopped
Mayonnaise

1. Chop meat in food processor and add relish, onion, celery and eggs.
2. Add a little salt and pepper. Fold in enough mayonnaise to make mixture spreadable.
3. Refrigerate. Spread on crackers or bread for sandwiches.

Chipped Beef Ball

1 (8 ounce) package cream cheese, softened
2 teaspoon horseradish
1 teaspoon prepared mustard
¼ teaspoon garlic powder
**1 (5 ounce) package smoked chipped beef, finely
    cut up**

1. In mixer bowl, blend cream cheese, horseradish, mustard and garlic powder. Roll into a ball.
2. Roll ball in the cut up chipped beef. (The best way to cut up chipped beef is with your scissors.) Serve with crackers.

Mexican Cheese Dip

1 pound cheddar cheese
1 (5 ounce) can evaporated milk
1 teaspoon cumin
1 tablespoon chili powder
1 (10 ounce) can tomatoes and green chilies

1. Melt cheese with the evaporated milk in double boiler.
2. In blender, mix together the cumin, chili powder and tomatoes and green chilies; adding a dash of garlic powder if you like.
3. Add tomato mixture to melted cheese; mixing well. Serve hot with chips.

Mexican Pick-Up Sticks

1 (7 ounce) can potato sticks
3 cans Spanish peanuts
2 (3 ounce) cans French fried onions
⅓ cup margarine, melted
1 (1.25 ounce) package taco seasoning dry mix

1. In a 9 x 13 inch baking dish, combine potato sticks, peanuts and fried onions.
2. Drizzle with melted margarine and stir. Sprinkle with taco seasoning and mix well.
3. Bake at 250 degrees for 45 minutes, stirring every 15 minutes.

Onion Guacamole Dip

1 (8 ounce) carton sour cream
1 package onion soup mix (dry)
2 (8 ounce) cartons avocado dip
2 green onions, chopped, tops too
½ teaspoon crushed dill weed

1. Mix all ingredients together and chill.
2. Serve with chips.

Tex-Mex Nachos

About 35 tortilla chips
1 (8 ounce) package shredded monterey jack
  cheese
2 tablespoon sliced jalapeno peppers
⅛ teaspoon chili powder
Bean Dip (Use Bean Dip recipe listed below.)

1. Arrange chips on 9 x 15 inch baking dish. Sprinkle with cheese. Top with jalapeno peppers; sprinkle with chili powder.
2. Broil 4 inches from heat until cheese melts.

Bean Dip

1 15 ounce) can Mexican-style chili beans
½ teaspoon ground cumin
½ teaspoon chili powder
¼ teaspoon dried oregano

1. Drain beans, reserving 2 tablespoons liquid. Combine beans, reserved liquid and remaining ingredients in container of food processor; pulse several times until beans are partially chopped.
2. Pour mixture into a small saucepan; cook over low heat, stirring constantly. until thoroughly heated. Serve with Tex-Mex Nachos.

Tuna-Avocado Dip

2 medium avocados
1 (6 ounce) can white tuna, drained
½ cup creamed cottage cheese
2 tablespoons lemon juice
Salt and pepper

1. Peel and cut avocados in chunks.
2. In mixer bowl, combine remaining ingredients and beat. Mixture will not be smooth; a little texture should remain.

Deluxe Pimento Cheese Spread

1 (16 ounce) package shredded sharp cheddar cheese
2 (4 ounce) jars diced pimentos, drained
1 cup picante sauce
¼ teaspoon freshly ground black pepper
3 tablespoons mayonnaise

1. In a large bowl, combine cheese, pimentos and picante sauce; mixing well.
2. Add pepper and mayonnaise, blending well.
3. Refrigerate. Spread on Wheatsworth crackers or use to make sandwiches.

Best Coffee Punch

1 gallon very strong coffee
½ cup sugar
3 tablespoons vanilla
2 pints half and half
1 gallon vanilla ice cream, softened

1. Add sugar to coffee (add more sugar if you like it sweeter); chill.
2. Add vanilla and half and half.
3. When ready to serve, combine coffee mixture and ice cream in punch bowl. Break up ice cream into chunks.

This is so good you will want a big glass of it
instead of a punch cup full.

Pineapple-Citrus Punch

1 (46 ounce) can pineapple juice, chilled
1 quart apple juice, chilled
1 (2 liter) bottle lemon-lime carbonated beverage,
chilled
1 (6 ounce) can frozen lemonade concentrate,
thawed
1 orange, sliced

1. Combine first 4 ingredients in a punch bowl.
2. Add orange slices for decoration.

Party Punch

1 (46 ounce) can pineapple juice
1 (46 ounce) can apple juice
3 quarts ginger ale, chilled

1. Freeze pineapple and apple juice in their cans.
2. One hour before serving, set out cans at room temperature
3. When ready to serve, place pineapple and apple juice in punch bowl and add the chilled ginger ale. Stir to mix.

Strawberry Punch

2 (10 ounce) boxes frozen strawberries, thawed
2 (6 ounce) cans frozen pink lemonade concentrate
2 (2 liter) bottles ginger ale, chilled

1. Process strawberries through blender. Pour lemonade into punch bowl and stir in strawberries.
2. Add chilled ginger ale and stir well. It would be nice to make an ice ring out of another bottle of ginger ale.

Creamy Strawberry Punch

1 (10 ounce) package frozen strawberries, thawed
½ gallon strawberry ice cream, softened
2 (2 liter) bottles ginger ale, chilled

1. Process strawberries through blender.
2. Combine strawberries, chunks of ice cream and the ginger ale in punch bowl. Stir and serve immediately.

Sparkling Cranberry Punch

Ice mold for punch bowl
Red food coloring
2 quarts cranberry juice cocktail, chilled
1 (6 ounce) can frozen lemonade concentrate, thawed
1 quart ginger ale, chilled

1. Pour water in a mold for the ice ring; add red food coloring to make the mold brighter and prettier.
2. Mix cranberry juice and lemonade in pitcher. Refrigerate until ready to serve.
3. When serving, pour cranberry mixture into punch bowl and add the ginger ale, stirring well. Add ice mold to the punch bowl.

Citrus Grove Punch

3 cups sugar
6 cups orange juice, chilled
6 cups grapefruit juice, chilled
1 ½ cups lime juice, chilled
1 liter ginger ale, chilled

1. In a saucepan, bring sugar and 2 cups water to a boil; cook for 5 minutes. Cover and refrigerate until cool.
2. Combine juices and sugar mixture; mix well.
3. Just before serving, stir in ginger ale. Serve over ice.

Cranberry Pineapple Punch

1 (48 ounce) bottle cranberry juice drink
1 (48 ounce) can pineapple juice
½ cup sugar
2 teaspoons almond extract
1 (2 liter) bottle ginger ale, chilled

1. Stir together first 4 ingredients until sugar dissolves. Cover and chill 8 hours.
2. When ready to serve, stir in ginger ale.

Easiest Grape Punch

½ gallon ginger ale
Red seedless grapes
Sparkling white grape juice, chilled

1. Make an ice ring of the ginger ale and seedless grapes.
2. When ready to serve, pour sparkling white grape juice in punch bowl with ice ring.

Sparkling white grape juice is great just by itself!

Ginger Ale Nectar Punch

1 (12 ounce) cans apricot nectar
1 (6 ounce) can frozen orange juice concentrate,
   thawed and undiluted
1 cup water
2 tablespoons lemon juice
1 (2 liter) bottle ginger ale, chilled

1. Combine first 4 ingredients; chill.
2. When ready to serve, stir in ginger ale.

Mocha Punch

4 cups brewed coffee
¼ cup sugar
4 cups milk
4 cups chocolate ice cream, softened

1. In a container, combine coffee and sugar; stir until sugar is dissolved. Refrigerate for 2 hours.
2. Just before serving, pour into a punch bowl. Add milk; mix well. Top with scoops of ice cream and stir well.

Instant Cocoa Mix

1 (8 quart) box dry milk powder
1 (12 ounce) jar non-dairy creamer
1 (16 ounce) can instant chocolate flavored drink mix
1 ¼ cups powdered sugar

1. Combine all ingredients and store in an airtight container.
2. To serve, use ¼ cup cocoa mix per cup of hot water.

Lemonade Tea

2 family size tea bags
½ cup sugar
1 (12 ounce) can frozen lemonade
1 quart ginger ale, chilled

1. Steep tea in 3 quarts of water; then mix with sugar and lemonade.
2. Add ginger ale just before serving.

Victorian Iced Tea

4 individual tea bags
4 cups boiling water
1 (11 ounce) can frozen cranberry-raspberry juice
   concentrate, thawed
4 cups cold water

1. Place tea bags in a teapot; add boiling water. Cover and steep for 5 minutes. Remove and discard tea bags. Refrigerate tea.
2. Just before serving, combine cranberry-raspberry concentrate and cold water in a 2 ½ quart pitcher; stir in tea. Serve with ice cubes.

Praline Coffee

3 cups hot brewed coffee
¾ cup half and half
¾ cup packed light brown sugar
2 tablespoons margarine
¾ cup praline liqueur

1. Cook first 4 ingredients in a large saucepan over medium heat, stirring constantly. Do not boil.
2. Stir in liqueur; serve with sweetened whipped cream.

Strawberry Smoothie

2 medium bananas, peeled and sliced
1 pint fresh strawberries, washed and quartered
1 (8 ounce) container strawberry yogurt
¼ cup orange juice

1. Place all ingredients in blender. Process until smooth.
2. Serve as is or over crushed ice.

Kahlua Frosty

1 cup Kahlua
1 pint vanilla ice cream
1 cup half and half
⅛ teaspoon almond extract
1 ⅔ cup crushed ice

1. Combine all ingredients in blender. Blend until smooth.
2. Serve immediately.

Kids' Cherry Sparkler

2 (6 ounce) jars red maraschino cherries, drained
1 (6 ounce) jars green maraschino cherries,
   drained
½ gallon distilled water
1 (2 liter) bottle cherry 7 UP, chilled

1. Place 1 red or green cherry in each compartment of 4 ice
   cube trays. Fill trays with distilled water; freeze for 8
   hours.
2. Serve soft drink over ice cubes.

Pink Fizz

**3 (6 ounce) cans frozen pink lemonade
  concentrate, undiluted**
1 (750 milliliter) bottles pink sparkling wine
**3 (2 liter) bottles lemon-lime carbonated beverage,
  divided, chilled**

1. Stir together concentrate, wine and 2 bottle carbonated
   beverage in an airtight container; cover and freeze 8 hours
   or until firm.
2. Let stand at room temperature 10 minutes; place in a
   punch bowl. Add remaining bottle carbonated beverage,
   stirring until slushy.

Wine Punch

2 (12 ounce) cans frozen limeade concentrate
4 limeade cans white wine, chilled
2 quarts ginger ale, chilled
Lime slices

1. Combine limeade, white wine and ginger ale in punch
   bowl.
2. Serve with an ice ring and lime slices.

Apple Party Punch

3 cups sparkling apple cider
2 cups apple juice
1 cup pineapple juice
½ cup brandy (optional)

1. Combine all ingredients and freeze 8 hours.
2. Remove punch from freezer 30 minutes before serving. Place in a small punch bowl and break into chunks. Stir until slushy.

Sparkling Punch

6 oranges, unpeeled and thinly sliced
1 cup sugar
2 (750 milliliter) bottles dry white wine
3 (750 milliliter) bottles sparkling wine, chilled

1. Place orange slices in a large nonmetallic container and sprinkle with sugar.
2. Add white wine; cover and chill at least 8 hours.
3. Stir in sparkling wine.

Champagne Punch

1 fifth dry white wine, chilled
1 cup apricot brandy
1 cup Triple Sec
2 bottles dry champagne, chilled
2 quarts club soda

1. In a large pitcher, combine white wine, apricot brandy and Triple Sec. Cover and keep chilled until ready to use.
2. At serving time, add champagne and club soda; stir to blend and place punch bowl.
3. Add an ice ring to punch bowl.

Banana-Mango Smoothie

1 cup cubed peeled ripe mango
1 sliced ripe banana
⅔ cup milk
1 teaspoon honey
¼ teaspoon vanilla extract

1. Arrange the mango cubes in a single layer on a baking sheet; freeze until firm, about 1 hour.
2. Combine frozen mango, banana, milk, honey and vanilla; pour into blender.
3. Process until smooth.

Tropical Smoothie

1 ½ heaping cups peeled, seeded ripe papaya
1 very ripe large banana
1 ½ heaping cups ripe cantaloupe, cut into chunks
1 (6 ounce) carton Yoplait Coconut Cream Pie
   Yogurt
¼ cup milk

1. Cut papaya into chunks. Place all ingredients in a blender and puree until smooth.
2. Pour into glasses; serve immediately.

Amaretto

3 cups sugar
2 ¼ cups water
1 pint vodka
3 tablespoons almond extract
1 tablespoon vanilla (not the imitation)

1. Combine sugar and water in a large pan. Bring mixture to a boil. Reduce heat. Let simmer 5 minutes, stirring occasionally. Remove from stove.
2. Add vodka, almond extract and vanilla. Stir to mix. Store in airtight jar.

Kahula

3 cups hot water
1 cup instant coffee granules
4 cups sugar
1 quart vodka
1 vanilla bean, split

1. In a large saucepan, combine hot water, coffee granules and sugar, mixing well. Bring to a boil; boil 2 minutes. Let cool.
2. Add vodka and vanilla bean. Pour into a bottle or jar and let set for 30 days before serving. Shake occasionally. (If you happen to have some Mexican vanilla, you can make "instant" Kahula by using 3 tablespoons of Mexican vanilla instead of the vanilla bean – and no waiting 30 days.)

Sweet Orange Fluff

1 ¾ cup milk
½ pint vanilla ice cream
⅓ cup frozen orange juice concentrate
1 teaspoon non-dairy creamer

1. In blender, combine all ingredients. Blend until smooth.

BREADS, BRUNCH & BREAKFAST

Cheesy Herb Bread

1 loaf French bread
½ teaspoon garlic powder
1 teaspoon marjoram leaves
1 tablespoon dried parsley leaves
1 stick margarine, softened
1 cup parmesan cheese

1. Slice bread into one inch slices. Combine garlic, marjoram, parsley and margarine. Spread mixture on bread slices and sprinkle with cheese.
2. Wrap in foil and bake at 375 degrees for 20 minutes. Unwrap and bake 5 more minutes.

Cheddar Butter Toast

1 stick margarine, softened
1 ¼ cups shredded cheddar cheese
1 teaspoon Worcestershire sauce
¼ teaspoon garlic powder
Thick sliced bread

1. Combine all ingredients together. Spread on thick sliced bread. Turn on broiler to toast; turn off broiler and leave in oven about 15 minutes.

Crispy Herb Bread

1 ½ teaspoons basil
1 teaspoon rosemary
½ teaspoon thyme
1 ½ sticks margarine, melted
1 package hot dog buns

1. Combine first 4 ingredients and let stand several hours at room temperature. Spread on buns and cut into strips.
2. Bake at 300 degrees for 15 to 20 minutes or until crisp.

Crunchy Bread Sticks

1 package hot dog buns
2 sticks margarine, melted
Garlic powder
Paprika

1. Take each half bun and slice in half lengthwise. Using a pastry brush, butter all bread sticks and sprinkle a light amount of garlic powder and a couple of sprinkles of paprika.
2. Place on cookie sheet and bake at 225 degrees for about 45 minutes.

This is an all-time favorite of our family.
I keep these made up in the freezer.
We have served these several times at our
Cancer Society luncheons and everybody loves them.

Garlic Toast

1 loaf French bread
1 tablespoon garlic powder
2 tablespoons dried parsley flakes
1 stick margarine, melted
1 cup parmesan cheese

1. Slice bread into 1 inch slices diagonally. In a small bowl combine rest of ingredients except cheese and mix well. Using a brush, spread mixture on bread slices and sprinkle with Parmesan cheese.
2. Place on cookie sheet and bake at 225 degrees for about 1 hour.

Mozzarella Loaf

1 (12 inch) loaf of French bread
12 slices mozzarella cheese
¼ cup grated parmesan cheese
¾ stick margarine, softened
½ teaspoon garlic salt

1. Cut loaf into 1 inch thick slices. Place slices of Mozzarella between bread slices.
2. Combine Parmesan cheese, margarine and garlic salt. Spread on each slice of bread. Reshape loaf, pressing firmly together and brush remaining margarine mixture on outside of loaf.
3. Bake at 375 degrees for 8 to 10 minutes.

Parmesan Bread Deluxe

1 loaf Italian bread
½ cup refrigerated creamy Caesar dressing
⅓ cup grated parmesan cheese
3 tablespoons finely chopped green onions

1. Cut 24 (½ inch thick) slices from bread. Reserve remaining bread for other use.
2. In small bowl, combine dressing, cheese and onion. Spread a teaspoon of dressing mixture onto each bread slice.
3. Place bread on baking sheet. Broil 4 inches from heat until golden brown. Serve warm.

Chile Bread

1 loaf Italian bread, unsliced
1 stick margarine, melted
1 (4 ounce) can diced green chilies, drained
¾ cup grated Monterey jack cheese

1. Slice bread almost all the way through. Combine melted margarine, chilies and cheese. Spread between bread slices.
2. Cover loaf with foil.
3. Bake at 350 degrees for 25 minutes.

Ranch French Bread

1 stick margarine, softened
1 tablespoon Hidden Valley Ranch dressing mix
1 loaf French bread

1. Cut loaf in half horizontally. Blend margarine and dressing mix.
2. Spread margarine mixture on bread. Wrap bread in foil.
3. Bake at 350 degrees 15 minutes.

Poppy Seed Bread

3 ¾ cups Bisquick
1 ½ cups shredded cheddar cheese
1 tablespoon poppy seed
1 egg, beaten
1 ½ cups milk

1. Combine all ingredients; beat vigorously 1 minute. Pour into a greased loaf pan.
2. Bake at 350 degrees for 50 to 60 minutes. Test for doneness with toothpick. Remove from pan and cool before slicing.

Quick Pumpkin Bread

1 (16 ounce) package pound cake mix
1 cup canned pumpkin
2 eggs
⅓ cup milk
1 teaspoon allspice

1. With mixer, combine and beat together all ingredients, blending well. Pour into a greased and floured 9 x 5 inch loaf pan.
2. Bake at 350 degrees for 1 hour. Use toothpick to check to be sure bread is done.
3. Cool and turn out onto cooling rack.

Butter Rolls

2 cups biscuit mix
1 (8 ounce) carton sour cream
1 stick butter, melted

1. Combine all ingredients and mix well. Spoon into greased muffin tins and fill only half full.
2. Bake at 400 degrees for 12 to 14 minutes or lightly brown.

Cheddar Cheese Loaf

3 ¾ cups baking (biscuit) mix
¾ cup shredded sharp cheddar cheese
1 ½ cups milk
2 small eggs
⅛ teaspoon ground red pepper

1. Combine baking mix and cheese. Add milk, eggs and pepper, stirring 2 minutes or until blended.
2. Spoon into a 9 x 5 inch Pam sprayed loaf pan.
3. Bake at 350 degrees for 45 minutes. Cool before slicing.

Popovers

2 cups flour
1 teaspoon salt
6 eggs, beaten
2 cups milk
Margarine

1. Combine flour and salt in bowl. Add eggs, milk and mix. Add dry ingredients; mixing well. The batter will be like heavy cream.
2. Coat popover pans with margarine and heat in oven. Fill each cup half full.
3. Bake at 425 degrees for 20 minutes. Reduce heat to 375 degrees and bake 25 more minutes. Serve immediately.

Cream Biscuits

2 cups flour
3 teaspoons baking powder
½ teaspoon salt
1 (8 ounce) carton whipping cream

1. Combine flour, baking powder and salt. In mixer bowl, beat the whipping cream only until it hold a shape. Combine the flour mixture and cream; mix with a fork.
2. Put dough on a lightly floured board and knead it for about 1 minutes. Pat dough to a ¾ inch thickness. Cut out biscuits with a small biscuit cutter.
3. Place on baking sheet; bake at 375 degrees for about 12 minutes or until lightly brown.

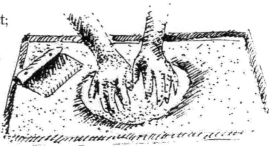

Lickety-Split

2 cups self-rising flour
4 tablespoons mayonnaise
1 cup milk

1. Mix all ingredients and drop by spoon on a cookie sheet.
2. Bake at 425 degrees until biscuits are golden brown.

Refrigerator Biscuits

1 (8 ounce) package cream cheese, softened
1 stick margarine, softened
1 cup self-rising flour

1. Beat cream cheese and margarine at medium speed with mixer for 2 minutes. Gradually add flour, beating at low speed, just until blended.
2. Spoon dough into miniature muffin pans, filling ⅔ full or you can refrigerate dough for up to 3 days.
3. Bake at 375 degrees for 15 minutes or until golden brown.

Sausage Biscuits

1 (8 ounce) package grated cheddar cheese
1 pound hot bulk pork sausage
2 cup Bisquick

1. Combine all three ingredients. Drop on ungreased cookie sheet.
2. Bake at 400 degrees until lightly brown. Serve hot.

Sour Cream Biscuits

2 cups flour, plus 1 tablespoon
3 teaspoon baking powder
½ teaspoon soda
½ cup shortening
1 (8 ounce) carton sour cream

1. Combine dry ingredients, adding a little salt and cut in shortening.
2. Gradually add sour cream. Mix lightly. Turn on lightly floured board and knead a few times. Roll to ½ inch thick. Cut with biscuit cutter and place on a greased baking sheet.
3. Bake at 400 degrees for 15 minutes or until lightly brown.

Spicy Cornbread Twists

⅓ stick margarine
⅓ cup cornmeal
¼ teaspoon red pepper
1 (11 ounce) can refrigerated soft breadsticks

1. Place margarine in a pie plate and melt in oven. Remove from oven.
2. On a piece of waxed paper, mix cornmeal and red pepper. Roll breadsticks in margarine and then in cornmeal mixture.
3. Twist the breadsticks as label directs and place on a cookie sheet. Bake at 350 degrees 15 to 18 minutes.

Hush Puppies

1 ¼ cups yellow corn meal
1 teaspoon salt
1 cup boiling water
½ onion, finely minced
1 eggs, beaten

1. Combine meal and salt. Bring water to boiling in sauce-pan; add meal and salt, stirring constantly. Cook until smooth and thick. Cool.
2. Add onion and egg; mix thoroughly.
3. Form into small balls; roll in flour and deep fry.

Cheddar Cornbread

2 (8 ½ ounce) packages corn bread-muffin mix
2 eggs, beaten
½ cup milk
½ cup plain yogurt
1 (14 ounce) can cream-style corn
½ cup shredded cheddar cheese

1. In a bowl, combine the cornbread mix, eggs, milk and yogurt until blended.
2. Stir in corn and cheese. Pour into a greased 9 x 13 inch baking dish.
3. Bake at 400 degrees for 18 to 20 minutes or until slightly browned.

Souper Sausage Cornbread

1 can golden corn soup
2 eggs
¼ cup milk
2 (6 ounce) packages corn muffin mix
¼ pound pork sausage, cooked, drained and crumbled

1. In bowl, combine soup, eggs and milk. Stir in muffin mix just until blended.
2. Fold in sausage. Spoon mixture into a greased 9x13 inch baking pan.
3. Bake at 400 degrees for about 20 minutes or until lightly brown.

Fried Cornbread

2 cups corn meal
1 ¼ teaspoons salt
½ teaspoon sugar
1 teaspoon baking powder
Oil

1. Combine dry ingredients, adding just enough boiling water to form a fairly stiff dough.
2. To fry, heat a little oil in a skillet. Take a heaping table-spoon of dough and place in skillet. Pat down with back of spoon so it can be turned over and fried on the top side. If the last few spoons of the cornbread get a little dry, add just a drip or two more water.
3. Brown on both sides and serve immediately.

This is really an old-time recipe and of course we try not to
fry things anymore – my husband just has to have this a
couple times a year with the old stand by "red beans".

Sour Cream Cornbread

1 cup self-rising cornmeal
1 (8 ounce) can cream-style corn
1 (8 ounce) carton sour cream
3 large eggs, lightly beaten
¼ cup oil

1. Heat a lightly greased 8 inch cast-iron skillet in a 400 degree oven.
2. Combine all ingredients, stirring just until moistened. Remove prepared skillet from oven and spoon batter into hot skillet.
3. Bake at 400 degrees for 20 minutes or until golden.

Cheese Muffins

3 ¾ cups buttermilk biscuit mix
1 ¼ cups grated cheddar cheese
1 egg, beaten
1 ¼ cups milk
Dash of chili powder

1. In large bowl, combine all ingredients and beat vigorously by hand.
2. Pour into greased muffin tins.
3. Bake at 325 degrees for 35 minutes.

Salad Muffins

⅓ **cup sugar**
⅓ **cup oil**
¾ **cup milk**
2 eggs
2 cups Bisquick mix

1. In mixing bowl, combine sugar, oil and milk. Beat in eggs and the Bisquick.
2. Mix well; mixture will be a little lumpy. Pour into greased muffin tins ⅔ full.
3. Bake at 400 degrees for about 10 minutes, until lightly browned.

Mayo Muffins

1 ¼ cup self-rising flour
3 tablespoons mayonnaise
1 cup whole milk

1. Mix all ingredients together and spoon into greased muffin tins.
2. Bake at 375 degrees for 20 minutes or until lightly browned.

Ginger Raisin Muffins

1 box Betty Crocker gingerbread mix
1 ¼ cups lukewarm water
1 egg
2 (1 ½ ounce) boxes seedless raisins

1. Combine gingerbread mix, water and egg, mixing well. Stir in raisins.
2. Pour into greased muffin tins filled half full.
3. Bake at 350 degrees for 20 minutes or when tested with a toothpick.

Kids' Corn Dog Muffins

2 (6 ounce) corn bread muffin mix
2 tablespoons brown sugar
2 eggs
1 cup milk
1 (8 ounce) can whole kernel corn, drained
5 hot dogs, chopped

1. In a bowl, combine corn bread mix and brown sugar. Combine eggs and milk; stir into dry ingredients. Stir in corn and hot dogs (batter will be thin).
2. Fill greased muffin cups ¾ full. Bake at 400 degrees for 16 to 18 minutes or until golden brown.

Orange French Toast

1 egg, beaten
½ cup orange juice
5 slices raisin bread
1 cup crushed graham crackers
2 tablespoons margarine

1. Combine egg and orange juice. Dip bread in mixture; then in crumbs.
2. Fry in margarine until brown.

French Toast

4 eggs
1 cup whipping cream
2 thick slices bread, cut into 3 strips
Powdered Sugar

1. Place a little oil in a skillet. Beat eggs, cream and a pinch of salt together. Dip bread into batter allowing batter to soak in. Fry bread in skillet until brown, turn and fry on the other side. Transfer to cookie sheet.
2. Bake at 325 degrees for about 4 minutes or until puffed.
3. Sprinkle with powdered sugar.

Breakfast Bake

1 pound hot sausage, cooked and crumbled
1 cup grated cheddar cheese
1 cup Bisquick
5 eggs, slightly beaten
2 cups milk

1. Place cooked and crumbled sausage in a Pam sprayed 9 x 13 inch baking dish. Sprinkle with cheese.
2. In mixing bowl, combine Bisquick, a little salt, and eggs; beat well. Add milk and stir until fairly smooth. Pour over sausage mixture.
3. Bake covered at 350 degrees for 35 minutes. You can mix this up the night before cooking. Refrigerate. To cook the next morning, add 5 minutes to cooking time.

This is a favorite of ours for over night guests or special enough for Christmas morning.

Christmas Breakfast

12 to 14 eggs, slightly beaten
1 pound sausage, cooked, drained, crumbled
2 cups whole milk
1 ½ cups grated cheddar cheese
1 (5.5 ounce) box seasoned croutons

1. Mix all ingredients together and pour into a 9 x 13 inch baking dish.
2. Bake covered at 350 degrees for 40 minutes. Let set for about 10 minutes before serving.

Bacon and Sour Cream Omelet

2 eggs
2 strips bacon, fried, drained and crumbled
⅓ cup sour cream
3 green onions, chopped
1 tablespoon margarine

1. Using a fork, beat eggs with 1 tablespoon water. Combine the bacon and sour cream. Saute the onions in remaining bacon drippings. Mix with the bacon-sour cream.
2. Melt margarine in an omelet pan. Pour in egg mixture and cook. When omelet is set, spoon sour cream mixture along the center and fold omelet out onto a warm plate.

Huevos Rancheros

8 eggs
3 tablespoons oil
4 corn tortillas
1 cup grated Monterrey jack cheese
Salsa

1. Lightly scramble 2 eggs at a time.
2. Fry tortillas in hot oil, drain. Place eggs on tortillas.
3. Top with cheese and roll up. Serve with salsa.

Sunrise Eggs

6 eggs
2 cups milk
1 pound sausage, cooked and browned
¾ cup grated Velveeta cheese
6 slices white bread, trimmed and cubed

1. Beat eggs and add milk, sausage and cheese.   Pour over bread and mix well.
2. Pour into a greased 9 x 13 inch baking pan and cover with foil.
3. Bake at 350 degrees for 20 minutes. Remove foil and turn oven up to 375 degrees; bake for another 10 minutes.

Mexican Breakfast Eggs

4 tablespoons margarine
9 eggs
3 tablespoons milk
5 tablespoons salsa
1 cup crushed tortilla chips

1. Melt margarine in skillet. In a bowl, beat eggs; add milk and salsa.
2. Pour into skillet and stir until eggs are lightly cooked.
3. Stir in tortilla chips. Serve hot.

Chiffon Cheese Souffle

12 slices white bread, crust trimmed off
2 (5 ounce) jars Old English cheese spread. softened
6 eggs, beaten
3 cups milk
1 ½ sticks margarine, melted

1. Spray Pam on a 9 x 13 inch baking dish. Cut each slice of bread into four triangles. Place a dab (with a knife) of cheese on each triangle and place triangles evenly in layers in baking dish. You could certainly make this in a soufflé dish if you have one.
2. Combine eggs, milk, margarine and a little salt and pepper. Pour over layers. Cover and chill 8 hours.
3. Remove from refrigerator 10 to 15 minutes before baking. Bake at 350 degrees, uncovered for one hour.

Wow! Is this ever good! It is light and fluffy, but still very rich. I think it is the Old English cheese that gives it that special cheese flavor.

Green Chili Squares

2 cups chopped green chilies
1 (8 ounce) package shredded sharp cheddar cheese
8 eggs, beaten
Salt and pepper
½ cup half and half

1. Place green chilies on bottom of a 9 x 13 inch baking pan. Cover with cheese.
2. Combine the eggs, salt, pepper and cream. Pour over chilies and cheese.
3. Bake at 350 degrees for 30 minutes. Let set at room temperature for a few minutes before cutting into squares.

Pineapple-Cheese Casserole

2 (20 ounce) cans unsweetened pineapple chunks (drained)
1 cup sugar, 5 tablespoons flour
1 ½ cups grated cheddar cheese
1 stack Townhouse or Ritz crackers, crushed
1 stick oleo, melted

1. Grease a 9 x 13 inch baking dish and layer in the following order; pineapple, sugar-flour mixture, grated cheese and cracker crumbs.
2. Drizzle margarine over casserole.
3. Bake at 350 degrees for 25 minutes or until bubbly.

This is really a different kind of recipe – but so good.
It can be served at brunch and it's great
with sandwiches at lunch.

Crabmeat Quiche

3 eggs, beaten
1 (8 ounce) carton sour cream
1 (6 ounce) can crabmeat, rinsed
½ cup grated Swiss cheese
1 (9 inch) pie shell

1. In bowl, combine eggs and sour cream. Blend in crabmeat and cheese; adding a little garlic salt and pepper.
2. Pour into a 9 inch unbaked pie shell.
3. Bake at 350 degrees for 35 minutes.

Apricot Casserole

4 (15 ounce) cans apricot halves, drained
1 (16 ounce) box light brown sugar *4 oz*
1 stack Ritz crackers, crumbled *½ stack dry*
1 stick margarine, sliced *¼ stick* *used*

¼ I know

1. Grease an 9 x 13 inch baking dish and line bottom with 2 cans of drained apricots.
2. Sprinkle half the brown sugar and half the cracker crumbs over apricots. Dot with half the margarine. Repeat layers.
3. Bake at 300 degrees for 1 hour.

Cinnamon Souffle

1 loaf cinnamon raisin bread
1 (20 ounce) can crushed pineapple, undrained
2 sticks margarine, melted
½ cup sugar
5 eggs, slightly beaten

1. Slice a very thin amount of the crusts off. Then tear the bread into small pieces and place in a buttered 9 x 13 inch baking dish.
2. Pour pineapple and juice over the bread and set aside. Cream together the margarine and sugar. Add eggs to creamed mixture, mixing well.
3. Pour the creamed mixture over the bread and pineapple. Bake uncovered for 40 minutes. One half cup chopped pecans could be added if you like.

Light and Crispy Waffles

2 cups biscuit mix
1 egg
½ cup oil
1 ⅓ cups club soda

1. Start waffle iron heating. Combine all ingredients in a mixing bowl and stir by hand. Pour just enough batter to cover waffle iron.
2. To have waffles for a "company weekend", make up all waffles. Freeze separately on cookie sheet, place in large baggies. To heat, place in a 350 degree oven for about 10 minutes.

Melon Boats

2 cantaloupes, chilled
4 cups red and green seedless grapes, chilled
1 cup mayonnaise
⅓ cup frozen concentrated orange juice, undiluted

1. Prepare each melon in 6 lengthwise sections, removing seeds and peeling. Place on separate salad plates on lettuce leaves. Heap grapes over and around the cantaloupe slices.
2. Combine mayonnaise and juice concentrate; mixing well. Ladle over fruit.

Curried Fruit Medley

1 (29 ounce) can sliced peaches
2 (15 ounce) cans pineapple chunks
1 (10 ounce) jar maraschino cherries
1 cup packed brown sugar
1 teaspoon curry powder
½ stick margarine, cut into pieces

1. Drain fruit; place in a 9 x 13 inch baking dish.
2. Combine brown sugar and curry; stirring well. Sprinkle over fruit; dot with margarine.
3. Bake covered at 350 degrees for 30 minutes or until thoroughly heated.

Treasure-Filled Apples

6 medium tart apples
½ cup sugar
¼ cup red hot candies
¼ teaspoon ground cinnamon

1. Cut tops off apples and set tops aside. Core apples to within ½ inch of bottom. Place in a greased 8 inch baking dish.
2. In a bowl, combine sugar, candies and cinnamon; spoon 2 tablespoons into each apple. Replace the tops. Spoon any remaining sugar mixture over the apples.
3. Bake, uncovered at 350 degrees for 30 to 35 minutes or until apples are tender, basting occasionally.

Ranch Sausage and Grits

1 cup quick-cooking grits
1 pound pork sausage
1 onion, chopped
1 cup salsa
1 (8 ounce) package shredded cheddar cheese,
divided

1. Cook grits according to directions; set aside. Cook and brown sausage and onion; drain. Combine grits, sausage mixture, salsa and half of the cheese. Spoon into a greased 2 quart baking dish.
2. Bake at 350 degrees for 15 minutes. Remove from oven and add remaining cheese on top of casserole.
3. Bake another 10 minutes. Serve hot.

Baked Grits

2 cups quick grits
4 cups water
2 cups milk
1 ½ sticks margarine
4 eggs, beaten

1. Stir grits in water over medium heat for about 5 minute. Add milk and margarine; cover and cook another 10 minutes.
2. Remove from heat and add beaten eggs.
3. Pour in a buttered casserole and bake covered at 350 degrees for 30 minutes.

Gingered Cream Spread

1 (8 ounce) package cream cheese, softened
1 stick unsalted margarine, softened
2 tablespoons milk
3 tablespoon finely chopped crystallized ginger

1. Combine all ingredients in mixer. Beat until creamy
2. Spread on your favorite fruit or nut breads.

Homemade Egg Substitute

6 egg whites
¼ cup instant nonfat dry milk powder
2 teaspoons water
2 teaspoons oil
¼ teaspoon ground turmeric

1. Combine all ingredients in electric blender and process 30 seconds.
2. Refrigerate. ¼ cup is the equivalent to one egg.

Blueberry Coffee Cake

1 (16 ounce) package blueberry muffin mix
⅓ cup sour cream
1 egg
⅔ cup powdered sugar
1 tablespoon water

1. Stir together the muffin mix, sour cream, egg and ½ cup water. Rinse blueberries and gently fold into batter. Pour into a Pam sprayed 7 x 11 inch baking dish.
2. Bake at 400 degrees for about 25 minutes. Cool.
3. Mix powdered sugar and 1 tablespoon water and drizzle over coffee cake.

Pineapple Coffee Cake

1 box butter cake mix
½ cup oil
4 eggs, slightly beaten
1 (8 ounce) can crushed pineapple, undrained

1. In mixer, combine cake mix, oil and eggs. Beat until well mixed.
2. Pour batter into a greased and floured 9x13 inch baking pan. Bake at 350 degrees for 45 to 50 minutes. Test with toothpick to make sure cake is done.
3. With a knife, punch holes in cake about 2 inches apart. Spread a can of pineapple pie filling over cake while cake is still hot.

SOUPS, SALADS & SANDWICHES

Spicy Tomato Soup

2 (10 ounce) cans tomato soup
1 (16 ounce) can Mexican stewed tomatoes
Sour cream
½ pound bacon, fried, drained and crumbled

1. In a saucepan, combine soup and stewed tomatoes and heat.
2. To serve, place a dollop of sour cream on each bowl of soup and sprinkle crumbled bacon over sour cream.

Beef Noodle Soup

1 pound lean ground beef
1 (46 ounce) can V8 juice
1 envelope onion soup mix
1 (3 ounce) package beef Ramen noodles
1 (16 ounce) package frozen mixed vegetables

1. In a large saucepan, cook beef over medium heat until no longer pink; drain. Stir in V8 juice, soup mix , contents of noodle seasoning packet and mixed vegetables.
2. Bring to a boil. Reduce heat; simmer, uncovered for 6 minutes or until vegetables are tender.
3. Return to a boil; stir in noodles. Cook for 3 minutes or until noodles are tender. Serve hot.

Broccoli Wild Rice Soup

1 (6 ounce) package chicken flavored wild rice mix
1 (10 ounce) package frozen chopped broccoli,
thawed
2 teaspoons dried minced onion
1 can cream of chicken soup, undiluted
1 (8 ounce) package cream cheese, cubed

1. In large saucepan, combine rice, contents of seasoning packet and 6 cups water. Bring to a boil, reduce heat, cover and simmer for 10 minutes, stirring once.
2. Stir in the broccoli and onion. Simmer 5 minutes.
3. Stir in soup and cream cheese. Cook and stir until cheese is melted.

This is hardy and a delicious soup – full of flavor.

Warm Your Soul Soup

3 (15 ounce) cans chicken broth
1 (10 ounce) can Italian stewed tomatoes,
undrained
½ cup onion, chopped
¾ cup chopped celery
½ (12 ounce) box Fettuccine

1. In large soup kettle, combine chicken broth, tomatoes, onion and celery. Bring to a boil; simmer until onion and celery are almost done.
2. Add pasta and cook the length of time according to pack-age directions. Season with a little salt and pepper.

Great flavor – great soup!

Crab Bisque

1 can cream of celery soup
1 can pepper pot soup
1 pint half and half
1 (6 ounce) can crabmeat, drained
A scant ⅓ cup sherry

1. Mix together soups and half and half.
2. Shred crabmeat and add.
3. Heat. Just before serving, add the sherry.

Clam Chowder

1 can New England clam chowder
1 can cream of celery soup
1 can cream of potato soup
1 (6.5 ounce) can chopped clams
1 soup can milk

1. Combine all ingredients in saucepan.
2. Heat and stir.

Cream of Cauliflower Soup

1 onion, chopped
½ teaspoon garlic powder
2 (14 ounce) cans chicken broth
1 large cauliflower, cut into small flowerets
1 ½ cup whipping cream

1. Saute onion and garlic powder in a tablespoon margarine. Stir in broth; bring to a boil. Add cauliflower; cook, stirring occasionally 15 minutes or until tender.
2. Process soup in batches in a blender until smooth; return to pan.
3. Stir in cream, adding a little salt and white pepper. Cook over low heat, stirring often, until thoroughly heated.

Cream of Zucchini Soup

1 pound fresh zucchini, grated
1 onion, chopped
1 (15 ounce) can chicken broth
½ teaspoon sweet basil
2 cups half and half

1. In saucepan, combine zucchini, onion, broth, basil, plus a little salt and pepper. Bring to a boil and simmer until soft. Empty into a food processor and puree.
2. Gradually add ½ cup of half and half and blend. Add ¼ teaspoon curry powder if you like the curry flavor.
3. Return zucchini mixture to saucepan and add remaining half and half. Heat, but to not boil.

Creamy Butternut Soup

4 cups cooked, mashed butternut squash
2 (14 ounce) cans chicken broth
½ teaspoon sugar
1 (8 ounce) carton whipping cream, divided
¼ teaspoon ground nutmeg

1. In saucepan, combine mashed squash, broth, sugar and a little salt. Bring to a boil and gradually stir in half of whipping cream Cook until thoroughly heated.
2. Beat remaining whipping cream. When ready to serve, place a dollop of whipped cream on soup and a sprinkle of nutmeg.

Easy Potato Soup

1 (16 ounce) package frozen hash brown potatoes
1 cup chopped onion
1 (14 ounce) can chicken broth
1 can cream of celery soup, 1 can cream of
   chicken soup
2 cups milk

1. In large saucepan, combine potatoes, onion and 2 cups water. Bring to a boil. Cover, reduce heat and simmer 30 minutes.
2. Stir in broth, soups and milk; heat thoroughly.
3. If you like, garnish with shredded cheddar cheese or diced, cooked ham.

Navy Bean Soup

3 cans navy beans, undrained
1 (14 ounce) can chicken broth
1 cup chopped ham
1 large onion, chopped
½ teaspoon garlic powder

1. In large saucepan, combine beans, broth, ham, onion and garlic powder. Add 1 cup water and bring to a boil. Simmer until onion is tender crisp.
2. Serve hot with corn bread.

Peanut Soup

2 cans cream of chicken soup
2 soup cans of milk
1 ¼ cups crunchy-style peanut butter

1. In a saucepan on medium heat, blend together the soup and milk.
2. Stir in peanut butter and heat until well blended.

Cold Cucumber Soup

3 medium cucumbers, peeled, seeded and cut into chunks
1 (14 ounce) can chicken broth
1 (8 ounce) carton sour cream
3 tablespoons fresh chives, minced
2 teaspoons fresh dill, minced

1. In blender, combine cucumbers, 1 cup of the chicken broth and a dash of salt. Cover and process until smooth. Transfer to medium bowl and stir in remaining chicken broth.
2. Whisk in sour cream, chives and dill. Cover and chill well before serving.
3. Garnish with dill sprig.

Chilled Squash Soup

2 pounds yellow squash, thinly sliced
1 onion, chopped
1 (14 ounce) can chicken broth
1 (8 ounce) package cream cheese, softened
¼ teaspoon freshly ground pepper

1. Combine first 3 ingredients in a saucepan; bring to a boil. Cover, reduce heat and simmer 10 minutes or until tender; cool.
2. Spoon half each of squash mixture and cream cheese into blender; process until smooth, stopping once to scrape down sides. Repeat procedure.
3. Stir in pepper and chill.

Avocado Cream Soup

4 ripe avocados, peeled and diced
1 ½ cups whipping cream
2 (14 ounce) cans chicken broth
1 teaspoon salt
¼ cup dry sherry

1. With blender, cream together half of the avocados and half the cream. Repeat with remaining avocados and cream.
2. Bring broth to a boil, reduce heat and stir in avocado puree. Add salt and sherry. chill thoroughly.
3. To serve, place in individual bowls and sprinkle a little paprika on top.

Asparagus Chiller

1 can condensed cream of asparagus soup
⅔ cup plain yogurt
½ cup chopped cucumber
2 tablespoon chopped red onion

1. Blend soup, yogurt and 1 soup can water. Add cucumber and onion.
2. Chill at least 4 hours and serve in chilled bowls.

Cold Strawberry Soup

2 ¼ cups strawberries
⅓ cup sugar
½ cup sour cream
½ cup heavy cream
½ cup light red wine

1. Place strawberries and sugar in blender and puree. Pour into a pitcher and stir in creams; blending well.
2. Add 1 ¼ cups water and the red wine. Stir and chill.

Strawberry Soup

1 ½ cups fresh strawberries
1 cup orange juice
¼ cup honey
½ cup sour cream
½ cup white wine

1. Combine all ingredients in blender. Process until strawberries are pureed.
2. Chill thoroughly. Stir before serving.

Broccoli Waldorf Salad

6 cups fresh broccoli florets
1 large red apple, chopped and unpeeled
½ cup golden raisins
½ cup chopped pecans
½ cup prepared coleslaw dressing

1. In a large bowl, combine the broccoli, apple, raisins and pecans.
2. Drizzle with the dressing and toss to coat. Refrigerate.
3. Serve in a pretty crystal bowl.

Broccoli Noodle Salad

1 cup almonds, toasted
1 cup sunflower seeds, toasted
2 (3 ounce) packages chicken Ramen noodles
  (uncooked)
1 package broccoli slaw
1 (8 ounce) bottle Italian salad dressing

1. You can toast the almonds and sunflower seeds by heating them in the oven at 275 degrees for about 10 minutes.
2. Break up Ramen noodles; mix with slaw, almonds and sunflower seeds.
3. Toss with the Italian salad dressing. Chill.

Broccoli-Green Bean Salad

1 large bunch broccoli, cut into florets
2 (15 ounce) cans cut green beans, drained
1 bunch fresh green onions, chopped, tops too
2 (6 ounce) jars marinated artichoke hearts,
   chopped and drained
1 ½ cups Hidden Valley original ranch dressing
   (made with mayonnaise)

1. Combine broccoli, green beans, onions and artichokes.
   Mixing well.
2. Add dressing and toss.
3. Chill 24 hours before serving.

Broccoli-Cauliflower Salad

1 small head cauliflower
3 stalks broccoli, 1 cup mayonnaise
1 tablespoon vinegar, 1 tablespoon sugar
1 bunch fresh green onions, chopped, tops too
8 ounces mozzarella cheese, cut in chunks

1. Cut up cauliflower and broccoli into bite-size flowerets.
   Combine mayonnaise, vinegar and sugar.
2. Combine cauliflower, broccoli, mayonnaise mixture, onions and cheese. Add a little salt if you like. Toss. Refrigerate.

Garlic Green Beans

3 cans whole green beans, drained
⅔ cup oil
½ cup vinegar
½ cup sugar
5 buttons garlic, finely chopped

1. Place green beans in container with lid. Mix together the oil, vinegar, sugar and garlic. Pour over beans. Sprinkle with a little salt and red pepper.
2. Let set overnight in refrigerator.

Summertime Mushroom Salad

1 (8 ounce) package cream cheese, softened
½ cup mayonnaise
½ teaspoon salt
1 bunch fresh green onion, chopped, tops too
4 cups fresh mushrooms, sliced

1. In mixer, cream together the cream cheese, mayonnaise and salt.
2. Gently mix in the onions and mushrooms. Chill and serve on a lettuce leaf.

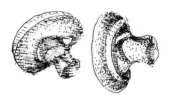

Winter Salad

1 (15 ounce) can cut green beans, drained
1 (15 ounce) can English peas, drained
1 (15 ounce) can whole kernel corn, drained
1 (15 ounce) can jalapeno black-eyed peas,
  drained
1 (8 ounce) bottle Italian dressing

1. Combine all vegetables in a large bowl. You can add some chopped onion and-or chopped bell pepper if you like.
2. Pour Italian dressing over vegetables.
3. Cover and refrigerate.

This is a great make-ahead salad and will stay fresh
at least a week.

Marinated Black-Eyed Peas

3 can Jalapeno black-eyed peas, drained
1 cup chopped celery
1 bunch fresh green onions, chopped, tops too
1 (4 ounce) jar pimentos, drained
1 (8 ounce) bottle Italian dressing

1. Mix all ingredients together and chill.
2. Let set several hours before serving.

Green Pea Salad

1 (16 ounce) bag frozen green peas
1 bunch fresh green onions, chopped, tops too
½ cup chopped celery
½ cup sweet pickle relish
Mayonnaise

1. Mix peas, onions, celery and relish together.
2. Add enough mayonnaise to hold salad together. Chill.

Sunflower Salad

2 apples, cored and chopped
1 cup seedless green grapes, halved
½ cup chopped celery
¾ cup chopped pecans
⅓ cup mayonnaise

1. Combine all ingredients and chill.

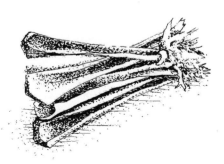

Avocado and Green Bean Salad

2 (15 ounce) cans French cut green beans, drained
8 green onions, chopped, tops too
¾ cup Italian salad dressing
2 avocados, chopped
1 (8 ounce) can artichoke hearts, drained and
**   chopped**

1. Place green beans and onions in a serving dish. Pour dressing over mixture and refrigerate several hours or overnight.
2. When ready to serve, stir in the avocado and artichoke hearts.

Cold Butterbean Salad

2 (10 ounce) packages frozen baby limas
1 (15 ounce) can shoe peg corn, drained
1 bunch fresh green onions, chopped, tops too
1 cup mayonnaise
2 teaspoons Hidden Valley Ranch seasoning

1. Cook beans according to directions, drain.
2. Add corn, onions, mayonnaise and seasoning; mix well.
3. Chill.

Nutty Green Salad

6 cups torn, mixed salad greens
1 medium zucchini, sliced
1 can sliced water chestnuts
½ cup peanuts
⅓ cup Italian salad dressing

1. Toss together the greens, zucchini, water chestnuts and peanuts.
2. When ready to serve, add salad dressing and toss.

Spinach and Apple Salad

1 (10 ounce) package fresh spinach
⅓ cup frozen orange juice concentrate, thawed
/4 cup mayonnaise
1 red apple, unpeeled and diced
5 slices bacon, fried and crumbled

1. Tear spinach into small pieces.
2. Mix orange juice concentrate and mayonnaise.
3. When ready to serve, mix spinach and apple (cut apple at the last minute); pour dressing over salad and top with bacon.

City Slicker Salad

2 (10 ounce) packages of fresh spinach
1 quart fresh strawberries, halved
½ cup slivered almonds, toasted
Poppy Seed Dressing

1. Tear spinach into smaller pieces and add the strawberries and almonds.
2. Refrigerate until ready to serve. Toss with Poppy Seed dressing.

Merry Berry Salad

1 (10 ounce) package mixed salad greens
2 apples, one red and one green, diced
1 cup shredded parmesan cheese
½ cup dried cranberries
½ cup slivered almonds, toasted

1. In a large salad bowl, toss the greens, apples, cheese, cranberries and almonds.
2. Drizzle poppy seed dressing over salad and toss.

Green and Red Salad

4 cups torn mixed salad greens
3 fresh green onions, chopped, tops too
2 medium red apples, diced (do not peel)
1 cup fresh raspberries
½ cup poppy seed dressing

1. In a bowl, toss the salad greens, onions and fruit.
2. Drizzle with dressing and toss.

Marinated Corn Salad

3 (15 ounce) cans whole kernel corn, drained
1 red bell pepper, chopped
1 cup chopped walnuts
¾ cup chopped celery
1 (8 ounce) bottle Italian salad dressing

1. In a bowl with a lid, combine corn, bell pepper, walnuts and celery. For a special little zip, I like to add several dashes of Tabasco.
2. Pour salad dressing over vegetables.
3. Refrigerate several hours before serving.

Mediterranean Potato Salad

2 pounds new red-skinned potatoes, cut into
   quarters
¾ to 1 cup Caesar dressing
½ cup grated Parmesan cheese
¼ cup chopped fresh parsley
½ cup chopped roasted red peppers

1. Cook potatoes in boiling water until fork-tender. Drain
2. Pour dressing over potatoes in large bowl.
3. Add cheese ,parsley and peppers. Toss lightly. Serve warm or chilled.

Pineapple Slaw

1 (8 ounce) can unsweetened pineapple tidbits,
   undrained
3 cups finely shredded cabbage
1 ½ cups unpeeled, chopped red delicious apple
½ cup chopped celery
¾ cup mayonnaise

1. Drain pineapple, reserving 3 tablespoons juice. Combine pineapple and next 3 ingredients in a large bowl. (Add dressing quickly after cutting apple so the apple will not darken.)
2. Combine reserved juice and mayonnaise; add to cabbage mixture, tossing tossing gently. Cover and chill.

Calypso Coleslaw

1 (16 ounce) package shredded cabbage
1 bunch green onions, sliced (tops too)
2 cups cubed cheddar cheese (or mozzarella cheese)
¼ cup sliced ripe olives
1 (15 ounce) can whole kernel corn with peppers,
   drained

1. Combine all slaw ingredients adding a few sprinkles of salt.

Dressing for Calypso Coleslaw

1 cup mayonnaise
2 tablespoons sugar
1 tablespoon prepared mustard
2 tablespoons vinegar

1. Combine dressing ingredients, mixing well.
2. Add dressing to slaw; toss. cover and refrigerate.

Homestyle Slaw

1 medium green cabbage, shredded
½ onion, chopped
⅓ cup sugar
1 cup mayonnaise
¼ cup vinegar

1. Toss cabbage and onion together. Salt and pepper to taste; sprinkle sugar over mixture.
2. Combine mayonnaise and vinegar. Pour over cabbage and onion. Toss and chill.

Easy Guacamole Salad

4 avocados, softened
1 (8 ounce) package cream cheese, softened
1 (10 ounce) can diced tomatoes and green chilies
1 ½ teaspoon garlic salt
About 1 tablespoon lemon juice

1. Peel avocados and mash with fork. In mixer, beat cream cheese until smooth; add the avocados and remaining ingredients. Mix well.
2. Place one of the avocado seeds in this salad and it will keep the mixture from turning dark. Of course, remove the seed when ready to serve.
3. This may be served on a lettuce leaf with a few Doritos beside the salad.

Terrific Tortellini Salad

2 (14 ounce) packages frozen cheese tortellini
1 green and 1 red bell pepper, diced
1 cucumber, chopped
1 (14 ounce) can artichoke hearts, rinsed and drained
1 (8 ounce) bottle creamy Caesar salad dressing

1. Prepare tortellini according to package directions; drain. Rinse with cold water; drain. Chill.
2. Combine tortellini and next 4 ingredients in a large bowl (you might want to add a little black pepper); cover and refrigerate at least 2 hours.

Special Rice Salad

1 package chicken Rice-a-Roni
¾ cup chopped green pepper
1 bunch fresh green onion, chopped, tops too
2 (6 ounce) jars marinated artichoke hearts, cut up
½ to ⅔ cup mayonnaise

1. Cook rice according to directions, omitting margarine. Drain. Cool.
2. Add remaining ingredients. Toss and chill.

This rice salad has lots of flavor!

Marinated Cucumbers

3 cucumbers, thinly sliced
2 (4 ounce) jars chopped pimientos, drained
⅔ cup oil
¼ cup white wine vinegar
1 (8 ounce) carton sour cream

1. Mix together cucumber and pimientos. Combine oil, vinegar and ½ teaspoon salt. Pour over cucumbers and chill 1 hour.
2. To serve, drain well and pour sour cream over cucumber and pimientos. Toss.

Marinated Brussel Sprouts

2 (10 ounce) boxes frozen brussel sprouts
1 cup Italian dressing
1 cup chopped green bell pepper
½ cup chopped onion

1. Pierce box of brussel sprouts and cook in microwave for 7 minutes.
2. Mix together the Italian dressing, bell pepper and onion.
3. Pour over brussel sprouts and marinate for at least 24 hours. Drain to serve.

Red Hot Onions

3 large purple onions
2 tablespoons Tabasco
3 tablespoon olive oil
3 tablespoons red wine vinegar

1. Slice onions thinly. Pour a cup of boiling water over onions and let stand 1 minute; drain.
2. Mix Tabasco, oil and vinegar and pour over onion rings in a shallow bowl. Refrigerate and let stand at least 3 hours. Drain to serve. Good with barbecue.

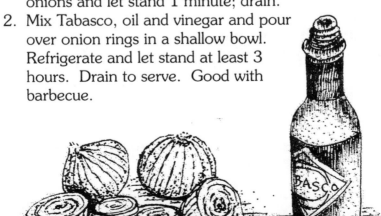

Black and Blue Eggs

12 large hard-cooked eggs
1 (4 ounce) package crumbled blue cheese
¼ cup half and half
2 tablespoons lime juice
2 tablespoons black caviar

1. Cut eggs in half lengthwise and carefully remove yolks. Mash yolks with a fork.
2. Add cheese, half and half and lime juice, stirring until smooth. Spoon back into egg whites.
3. Top with caviar. Refrigerate.

Chicken Salad

3 cups finely chopped cooked chicken breasts
1 ½ cups chopped celery
½ cup sweet pickle relish
2 hard-boiled eggs, chopped
¾ cup mayonnaise

1. Combine all ingredients and several sprinkles of salt and pepper.

Adding ½ cup chopped pecans gives
the chicken salad a special taste.

Creamy Orange Salad

1 (6 ounce) package orange gelatin
1 (8 ounce) package cream cheese, softened
1 (14 ounce) can sweetened condensed milk
1 (8 ounce) carton Cool Whip
2 (11 ounce) cans mandarin orange slices, drained

1. In bowl, dissolve gelatin in 1 ¼ cup boiling water. In mixing bowl, beat cream cheese until fluffy. Gradually blend in hot gelatin, beating on low speed until smooth.
2. Stir in condensed milk; refrigerate until mixture begins to thicken. Fold in Cool Whip and orange slices.
3. Spoon into a 9 x 13 inch glass dish. Refrigerate 4 hours before serving.

Fantastic Fruit Salad

2 (11 ounce) cans mandarin oranges
2 (15 ounce) cans pineapple chunks
1 (16 ounce) carton frozen strawberries, thawed
1 can peach pie filling
1 can apricot pie filling

1. Drain oranges, pineapple and strawberries. Combine all ingredients and fold together gently.
2. If you like you can add 2 sliced bananas to this salad.

Peachy Fruit Salad

2 cans peach pie filling
1 (20 ounce) can pineapple chunks, drained
1 (11 ounce) can mandarin oranges, drained
1 (8 ounce) jar maraschino cherries, drained
1 cup miniature marshmallows

1. Combine all ingredients in large bowl. Fold together gently. Refrigerate.
2. Serve in a pretty crystal bowl. (Bananas can be added if you like.)

Fluffy Fruit Salad

2 (20 ounce) can pineapple tidbits, drained
1 (16 ounce) can whole cranberry sauce
2 (11 ounce) cans mandarin oranges, drained
½ cup chopped pecans
1 (8 ounce) carton Cool Whip

1. In bowl, combine pineapple, cranberries, oranges, and pecans.
2. Fold in Cool Whip.
3. Serve in a pretty crystal bowl.

Cherry Salad

1 can cherry pie filling
1 (20 ounce) can crushed pineapple, drained
1 can sweetened condensed milk
1 cup miniature marshmallows
1 cup chopped pecans
1 (8 ounce) carton Cool Whip

1. In large bowl, combine pie filling, pineapple, condensed milk, marshmallows and pecans.
2. Fold in Cool Whip, chill and serve in a pretty crystal bowl.
3. You can add a couple drops of red food coloring if you like a brighter color.

Cottage Cheese and Fruit Salad

1 (16 ounce) carton small curd cottage cheese
1 (6 ounce) package orange gelatin
2 (11 ounce) cans mandarin oranges, drained
1 (20 ounce) can chunk pineapple, drained
1 (8 ounce) carton Cool Whip

1. Sprinkle gelatin over cottage cheese, mixing well. Add oranges and pineapple, mixing well.
2. Fold in Cool Whip. Chill. Pour into a pretty crystal bowl.

Angel Salad

1 (8 ounce) package cream cheese, softened
½ cup sugar
1 (16 ounce) can chunky fruit cocktail, drained
1 (15 ounce) can pineapple chunks, drained
1 (8 ounce) carton Cool Whip

1. With mixer, beat cream cheese and sugar until creamy. Add fruit, mixing gently.
2. Fold in Cool Whip. Pour into a crystal bowl and refrigerate.

Strawberry Rhubarb Salad

2 cups diced frozen rhubarb
¾ cup sugar
¼ cup water
1 (3 ounce) package strawberry gelatin
1 ½ cups Cool Whip

1. In a saucepan, bring rhubarb, sugar and water to a boil. Reduce heat, simmer, uncovered for 3 to 5 minutes or until rhubarb is softened.
2. Remove from heat; stir in gelatin until dissolved. Pour into a bowl. Refrigerate for 30 minutes or until partially set.
3. Fold in Cool Whip. Pour into a serving dish. Chill until firm.

Peaches 'N Cream Salad

1 (6 ounce) package lemon gelatin
1 cup boiling water
1 (8 ounce) package cream cheese, softened
1 (8 ounce) carton Cool whip
1 can peach pie filling, 1 can sliced peaches,
   drained

1. In mixing bowl, combine gelatin and boiling water. Mix well and pour half into a separate bowl and set aside.
2. With the gelatin in mixing bowl, add the cream cheese and begin beating very slowly; beat until smooth and creamy. Place in refrigerator just until it begins to thicken but not set. Fold in Cool Whip and pour into a 9 x 13 inch glass dish. Refrigerate until set.
3. With remaining gelatin, mix in the peach pie filling and sliced peaches. Pour over first layer. Refrigerate several hours.

Butter Mint Salad

1 (6 ounce) box lime gelatin
1 (20 ounce) can crushed pineapple, undrained
½ (10 ounce) bag miniature marshmallows
1 (8 ounce) carton Cool Whip
1 (8 ounce) bag buttermints, crushed

1. Pour dry gelatin over pineapple. Add marshmallows and let set overnight.
2. Fold in Cool whip and buttermints. Pour into a 9 x 13 inch dish and freeze.

This salad is so good served with the Hawaiian Chicken.

Cream Cheese and Mango Salad

1 (15 ounce) can mangos
1 (6 ounce) packages lemon gelatin
2 (8 ounces) cream cheese, softened

1. Drain juice from mangos. Combine juice and enough water to make 1 ⅓ cups liquid. Bring to a boil and add gelatin. Stir until well dissolved.
2. In mixing bowl, cream together the mangos and cream cheese.
3. Mix into hot gelatin and pour into muffin tins or a mold.

Tropical Mango Salad

2 (15 ounce) cans mangoes, save juice
1 (6 ounce) package orange gelatin
1 (8 ounce) package cream cheese, softened
½ (8 ounce) carton Cool Whip

1. Place all mango slices on a dinner plate and with a knife and fork, cut slices into bite-size pieces. Place 1 ½ cups of the mango juice (if not that much juice, add water to make 1 ½ cups) in a saucepan and bring to boiling point. Pour over gelatin in mixer bowl and mix well.
2. Add cream cheese and start mixer very slowly. Gradually increase speed until cream cheese is mixed into gelatin. Pour in mango pieces. Place in refrigerator until it is lightly congealed.
3. Fold in Cool Whip. Pour into a 7 x 11 inch dish. Chill.

Luscious Strawberry Salad

1 (6 ounce) package strawberry gelatin
2 (10 ounce) boxes frozen strawberries, thawed
3 bananas, sliced
1 (8 ounce) carton sour cream

1. Dissolve gelatin in 1 ¼ cups boiling water, mixing well. Add strawberries and bananas. Pour half mixture in a 7 x 11 inch dish, leaving all the bananas in the bottom layer. Chill until firm
2. Spread sour cream over firm gelatin. Add remaining gelatin over sour cream.
3. Refrigerate until firm.

Holiday Cheer

2 cups ginger ale
1 (6 ounce) package orange gelatin
1 cup wine
1 (9 ounce) package condensed mincemeat
1 cup chopped pecans

1. Heat ginger ale and stir into gelatin; mixing well.
2. Add wine, mincemeat and pecans. Pour into a 9 x 13 inch glass dish.
3. Refrigerate.

Pistachio Salad (or Dessert)

1 (20 ounce) can crushed pineapple, undrained
1 (3 ounce) package instant pistachio pudding mix
2 cups miniature marshmallows
1 cup chopped pecans
1 (8 ounce) carton Cool Whip

1. Place pineapple in a large bowl. Sprinkle with dry pudding mix.
2. Add marshmallows and pecans. Fold in Cool Whip. Pour into a crystal serving dish.
3. Refrigerate.

Serendipity Salad

1 (6 ounce) package raspberry gelatin
1 (16 ounce) can fruit cocktail, undrained
1 (8 ounce) can crushed pineapple, undrained
2 bananas, cut into small chunks
1 cup miniature marshmallows

1. Dissolve gelatin in 1 cup boiling water, mixing well.
2. Add fruit cocktail and pineapple. Chill until gelatin begins to thicken.
3. Add bananas and marshmallows. Pour into sherbet dishes. Cover with plastic wrap and refrigerate. You could also pour salad into a 7 x 11 inch glass dish and cut into squares to serve.

Pink Salad

1 (6 ounce) package raspberry gelatin
1 (20 ounce) can crushed pineapple, reserve juice
1 cup cream style cottage cheese
1 (8 ounce) carton Cool Whip
¼ cup chopped pecans

1. Place gelatin in large bowl. Heat juice from pineapple and enough water to make 1 ¼ cups. Pour over gelatin and mix well.
2. Cool in refrigerator until gelatin just begins to get thick. Fold in cottage cheese, Cool Whip and pecans.
3. Pour into molds or a 9 x 13 inch dish. Refrigerate.

Divinity Salad

1 (6 ounce) package lemon gelatin
1 (8 ounce) package cream cheese
¾ cup chopped pecans
1 (15 ounce) can crushed pineapple, undrained
1 (8 ounce) carton Cool Whip

1. With mixer, mix gelatin with 1 cup boiling water until well dissolved.
2. Add cream cheese, beat slowly to start with, beat until smooth. Add pecans and pineapple. Cool in refrigerator until nearly set.
3. Fold in Cool Whip. Pour into a 9 x 13 inch dish. Refrigerate.

Purple Lady Salad

1 (6 ounce) box grape gelatin
1 can blueberry pie filling
1 (20 ounce) can crushed pineapple, undrained
1 cup miniature marshmallows
1 cup chopped pecans

1. In large bowl, place gelatin and pour 1 cup boiling water over gelatin, mixing well.
2. Add blueberry pie filling and pineapple. Place in refrigerate until gelatin begins to thicken; then stir in marshmallows and pecans. Pour into a 9 x 13 inch glass dish.
3. Refrigerate. (To make a completely different salad, you can fold in an 8 ounce carton of Cool Whip when mixture begins to congeal.)

Cherry Cranberry Salad

1 (6 ounce) package cherry gelatin
1 cup boiling water
1 can cherry pie filling
1 (16 ounce) can whole cranberry sauce

1. In mixing bowl, combine cherry gelatin and boiling water; mixing until gelatin is dissolved.
2. Mix pie filling and cranberry sauce into gelatin.
3. Pour into a 9 x 13 in dish and refrigerate.

Creamy Cranberry Salad

1 (6 ounce) package cherry gelatin
1 (8 ounce) carton sour cream
1 (16 ounce) can whole cranberry sauce
1 (15 ounce) can crushed pineapple, undrained

1. Dissolve gelatin in 1 ¼ cups boiling water, mixing well.
2. Stir in remaining ingredients and pour into a 7 x 11 inch glass dish. Refrigerate until firm.

Cashew Salad

1 (6 ounce) package lemon gelatin
1 quart vanilla ice cream
1 (15 ounce) can fruit cocktail, drained
1 cup chopped cashew nuts

1. Dissolve gelatin in 1 cup boiling water and stir in ice cream. Blend until ice cream is melted.
2. Add fruit cocktail and cashew nuts; mix well.
3. Pour into an 7 x 11 inch glass dish. Refrigerate overnight.

Cinnamon Apple Salad

1 cup cinnamon red hot candies
1 (6 ounce) package cherry gelatin
1 (16 ounce) jar applesauce
1 cup chopped pecans
Sour cream

1. Heat cinnamon red hots in 1 ¼ cups boiling water until candy melts. While mixture is still hot, pour over gelatin and mix well.
2. Add applesauce and chopped pecans, mixing well.
3. Pour into 7 x 11 inch glass dish and refrigerate until firm. When serving, cut in squares and place a dollop of sour cream on top of salad.

Frozen Dessert Salad

1 (8 ounce) package cream cheese, softened
1 cup powdered sugar
1 (10 ounce) box frozen strawberries, thawed
1 (15 ounce) can crushed pineapple, drained
1 (8 ounce) carton Cool Whip

1. In mixer bowl, beat together the cream cheese and sugar.
2. Fold in remaining ingredients. This will be even better if you stir in ¾ cup chopped pecans.
3. Pour into a 9 x 9 inch pan. Freeze. Cut into squares to serve.

Frozen Cherry Salad

1 (8 ounce) package cream cheese, softened
1 (8 ounce) carton Cool Whip
1 can cherry pie filling
2 (11 ounce) cans mandarin oranges, drained
¾ cup coarsely chopped pecans

1. With mixer, beat cream cheese until smooth. Fold in Cool Whip.
2. Stir in pie filling, oranges and pecans.
3. Transfer to a 9 x 5 inch loaf pan. Cover and freeze overnight. Remover from freezer 15 minutes before slicing. Serve on a lettuce leaf.

Frozen Cranberry-Pineapple Salad

1 (20 ounce) can crushed pineapple, drained
2 (16 ounce) cans whole cranberry sauce
1 (8 ounce) carton sour cream
¾ cup chopped pecans

1. In large bowl, combine all ingredients.
2. Pour into a Pam sprayed 8 x 11 inch glass dish.
3. Freeze several hours before serving.

Hot Bunwiches

8 hamburger buns
8 slices Swiss cheese
8 slices ham
8 slices turkey
8 slices American cheese

1. Lay out all 8 buns. On the bottom, place the slices of Swiss cheese, ham, turkey and American cheese. Place the top bun over the American cheese. Wrap each bunwich individually in foil and place in freezer.
2. When ready to serve, take out of freezer 2 to 3 hours before serving.
3. Heat in a 325 degree oven for about 30 minutes. Serve hot.

Grilled Bacon and Banana Sandwiches

Peanut butter
8 slices English muffins
2 bananas
8 slices bacon, crispy cooked
Margarine, softened

1. Spread a layer of peanut butter over 8 slices of muffins. Slice bananas and arrange on top of 4 slices.
2. Place 2 strips bacon on each of the 4 slices. Top with remaining muffin slices. Spread top slice with margarine.
3. Brown sandwiches, margarine side down. Turn, spread margarine and cook the other side until golden brown. Serve hot.

Reuben Sandwiches

For each sandwich: 2 slices rye bread
1 slice Swiss cheese
A generous slice corned beef
2 tablespoons sauerhraut
Dijon mustard

1. Butter one slice of bread on one side. Place butter side down in skillet over low heat.
2. Layer on bread: cheese , corned beef, sauerkraut and spread mustard on one side of other slice; butter opposite side. Place butter side up on sauerkraut.
3. Cook until bottom is browned, turn carefully and brown other side.

Pizza Sandwich

1 (14 ounce) package English muffins
1 pound bulk sausage, cooked and drained
1 ½ cups pizza sauce
1 (4 ounce) can mushrooms, drained
1 (8 ounce) package shredded Mozzarella cheese

1. Split muffins.
2. Layer ingredients on each muffin half, ending with the cheese.
3. Broil until cheese melts.

Turkey Asparagus Sandwiches

4 (1 ounce) slices cheddar cheese
2 English muffins, split and toasted
½ pound thinly sliced turkey
1 (15 ounce) can asparagus spears
1 package hollandaise sauce mix

1. Place a cheese slice on each muffin half; top evenly with turkey.
2. Cut asparagus spears to fit muffin halves and top each sandwich with 3 or 4 asparagus spears; reserve remaining asparagus for another use.
3. Prepare sauce mix according to package directions; pour evenly over sandwiches. Sprinkle with paprika if desired.

Turkey-Cranberry Croissant

1 (8 ounce) package cream cheese, softened
¼ cup orange marmalade
6 large croissants, split
Lettuce leaves
1 pound thinly sliced cooked turkey
¾ cup whole berry cranberry sauce

1. Beat together the cream cheese and orange marmalade. Spread evenly on cut sides of croissants.
2. Place lettuce leaves and turkey on croissant bottoms; spread with cranberry sauce.
3. Cover with croissant tops.

Provolone Pepper Burgers

⅓ cup finely cubed provolone cheese
¼ cup diced roasted red peppers
¼ cup finely chopped onion
1 pound lean ground beef
4 hamburger buns, split

1. In a bowl, combine the cheese, red peppers, onion and a little salt and pepper. Add beef; mix well. Shape into 4 patties.
2. Grill covered, over medium-hot heat for 5 minutes on each side or until meat is no longer pink.
3. Add your favorite lettuce, tomatoes, etc.

Meatball Hoagies

1 small onion, diced
1 small green bell pepper, diced
1 (15 ounce) can sloppy Joe sauce
30 to 32 frozen cooked meatballs
4 hoagie buns

1. Saute onion and pepper in 1 tablespoon oil.
2. Add sauce and meatballs; cook 10 minutes or until thoroughly heated, stirring often.
3. Spoon evenly onto hoagie buns.

Sloppy Joes

1 pound lean ground beef
1 can Italian tomato soup
2 teaspoons Worcestershire
⅛ teaspoon black pepper
6 hamburger buns, split and toasted

1. In skillet, cook beef until browned, stirring to separate meat. Spoon off fat.
2. Add soup, ¼ cup water, Worcestershire and pepper. Heat thoroughly, stirring often.
3. Serve on buns.

Party Sandwiches

1 (8 ounce) package cream cheese, softened
⅓ cup chopped stuffed olives
2 tablespoons olive juice
⅓ cup chopped pecans
6 slices bacon, cooked and crumbled

1. Beat cream cheese with mixer until smooth.
2. Add all other ingredients.
3. Spread on party rye bread.

Spinach Sandwiches

**1 (10 ounce) package chopped spinach, thawed
  and well drained
1 cup mayonnaise
1 (8 ounce) carton sour cream
½ cup finely minced onion
1 envelope Knorr's dry vegetable soup mix**

1. Make sure spinach is WELL drained. Add remaining ingredients, mixing well. (If you like, ¾ cup finely chopped pecans can be added.)
2. Let this spread stay refrigerated for 3 to 4 hours before making sandwiches.
3. To make sandwiches, use thin white bread.

Orange Cheese Spread

**2 (8 ounce) packages cream cheese, softened
½ cup powdered sugar
1 tablespoon grated orange peel
2 tablespoons Grand Marnier
2 tablespoons frozen orange juice concentrate,
  undiluted**

1. Blend all ingredients together in mixer until smooth. Refrigerate.
2. Spread on dessert breads to make sandwiches. This spread is great on poppy seed buns.
3. This can also be used as a dip for fruit.

Hot and Sweet Mustard

4 ounces dry mustard
1 cup vinegar
3 eggs
1 cup sugar

1. Soak dry mustard in vinegar overnight.
2. Beat eggs and sugar together; then add to vinegar mustard mixture. In top of double boiler, cook over low heat for approximately 15 minutes, stirring constantly. Mixture will resemble a custard consistency.
3. Pour immediately into jars. Store in refrigerator. Serve with ham.

Great to keep in the refrigerator for ham sandwiches.

Remoulade Mayonnaise

1 cup mayonnaise
½ cup chunky salsa
¼ cup sweet pickle relish
1 teaspoon Dijon mustard
1 tablespoon horseradish

1. Combine all ingredients, mixing well. This is a great spread for beef or ham sandwiches.
2. Refrigerate.

SANDWICHES EXTRAORDINAIRE

Here are some new or different combinations for sandwiches you may not have tried before. You'll get some "ooh's" and "aah's" and maybe even a raised eyebrow or two.

Sandwich Inspiration I
Pumpernickel bread
Mayonnaise
Deli sliced corned beef
Slices of Swiss cheese
Lettuce

Sandwich Inspiration II
Dark rye bread
2 slices corned beef
2 slices Swiss cheese
4 tablespoons sauerkraut
Russian dressing

Sandwich Inspiration III
Hoagie Rolls
Grey Poupon mustard
Slices of pastrami
Slices of Mozzarella cheese
Deli cold slaw

Sandwich Inspiration IV
Pita bread
Ham slices
Mozzarella cheese slices
Slices of sweet pickles
Bean sprouts and mayonnaise

Sandwich Inspiration V
Rye bread
Slices Mozzarella cheese
Deli ham salad
Avocado slices
Lettuce

Sandwich Inspiration VI
French bread slices
Turkey and deli beef slices
Slices of American cheese
Slices of Monterey jack cheese
Lettuce with mayonnaise

Sandwich Inspiration VII
Whole wheat bread
Slices of American cheese
Deli shrimp or crab salad
Slices of avocados
Lettuce

Sandwich Inspiration VIII
Kaiser Rolls
Spread with softened cream cheese
Deli egg salad
Slices of dill pickles
Bean sprouts

Sandwich Inspiration X

Multi-grain bread
Deli turkey breasts
Slices havarti cheese
Fresh spinach
Garlic mayonnaise

Sandwich Inspiration XI

Pumpernickle bread
Deli roast beef
Fresh spinach
Tomato slices
Quick guacamole

Sandwich Inspiration XII

French rolls
Thin slices brie cheese
Deli turkey breast slices
Chutney spread
Mayonnaise

Sandwich Inspiration XIII

Kaiser rolls
Grilled chicken breasts
Canned pineapple slices
Leaf lettuce
Sesame-ginger mayonnaise

Sandwich Inspiration IX

Slices marble rye bread
Slices deli peppered roast beef
Slices sweet onion,
   separated into rings
Leaf lettuce
Horseradish mayonnaise

Sandwich Inspiration XX

Honey nut bread
Crisp cooked bacon slices
Tomato Slices
Bibb lettuce
Remoulade mayonnaise

Special Sandwich Spreads:

Horseradish Mayonnaise:
½ cup mayonnaise
1 tbsp. chopped fresh chives
1 tbsp. prepared horseradish
⅛ tsp. seasoned salt
Combine ingredients. Refrigerate.

Garlic Mayonnaise:
⅔ cup mayonnaise
1 tbsp. chopped roasted garlic
1 tsp. finely chopped onion
⅛ tsp. salt
Combine ingredients refrigerate

Remoulade Mayonnaise:
½ cup mayonnaise
2 tbsp. chunky salsa
1 tsp. chopped fresh parsley
1 tsp. sweet pickle relish
1 tsp. Dijon mustard

Chutney Spread:
⅓ cup peach preserves
½ cup chopped fresh peaches
2 tsp. finely chopped green onion
½ tsp. balsamic vinegar
¼ tsp. crushed red pepper flake

Sesame-Ginger Mayonnaise:
⅔ cup mayonnaise
1 tbsp. honey
1 tbsp. toasted sesame seeds
2 tsp. grated fresh gingerroot

Quick Guacamole:
1 package onion soup mix (dry)
2 (8 ounce) cartons avocado dip
2 green onions, chopped, tops too
½ tsp. crushed dill weed

BURGERS WITH A FLAIR

Basic Burger

1 ¼ pounds ground chuck
1 egg
2 teaspoons Worcestershire sauce
½ teaspoon salt
¼ teaspoon black pepper

1. Mix ground chuck with egg, Worcestershire, salt and pepper. Form into 4 or 5 patties about ½ inch thick and about 4 inches in diameter. Cook on a grill for about 5 to 6 minutes on each side or in a skillet for about 4 to 5 minutes on each side. (Ground beef should never be cooked rare.)
2. You will need 4 buns which you will want to toast and spread with mayonnaise or mustard.
3. You will also want lettuce, tomatoes and a slice of onion for your hamburger.

Here are some suggested additions to your basic hamburger – for a little change of taste:

Super Hamburger I
Add 2 slices of crisp, cooked bacon, American cheese and Swiss cheese slices for each bun.

Super Hamburger II
Spread some deli prepared guacamole and sliced hot peppers.

Super Hamburger III
Instead of lettuce, spread about 3 tablespoons of deli prepared slaw and a few sunflower seeds.

Super Hamburger IV
Add thin slices of apples and some chopped peanuts.

Super Hamburger V

Add thin slices of cucumber and sliced olives.

Super Hamburger VI

Instead of American cheese, use Monterey jack cheese.
Instead of mayonnaise or mustard, use prepared
guacamole as a spread.

Super Hamburger VII

Add slices of pastrami and slices of Mozzarella cheese.

Super Hamburger VIII

Add slices of salami and slices of Swiss cheese.

Super Hamburger VI

Add slices of avocados (mayonnaise, not mustard) and
slices of crisp, cooked bacon.

VEGETABLES
&
SIDE DISHES

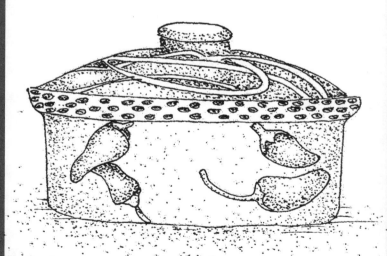

Asparagus Bake

4 (10.5 ounce) cans asparagus
3 eggs, hard-boiled and sliced
⅓ cup milk
1 ½ cups grated cheddar cheese
1 ¼ cups cheese cracker crumbs

1. Place asparagus in 7 x 11 inch baking dish. Place hard-boiled eggs on top. Pour milk over casserole.
2. Sprinkle cheese on top, then add the cracker crumbs.
3. Bake uncovered at 350 degrees for 30 minutes.

Almond Asparagus

⅓ cup margarine
1 to 1 ½ pounds fresh asparagus
⅔ cup slivered almonds
1 tablespoon lemon juice

1. Melt margarine in skillet and add the asparagus and almonds. Saute 3 to 4 minutes.
2. Cover and steam about 2 minutes. or until tender crisp.
3. Sprinkle lemon and a little salt and pepper over asparagus. Serve hot.

Asparagus Caesar

3 (15 ounce) cans asparagus spears, drained
½ stick margarine, melted
3 tablespoons lemon juice
½ cup grated parmesan cheese

1. Place asparagus in a 2 quart baking dish. Drizzle on margarine and lemon juice. Sprinkle with cheese (and a little paprika if you like).
2. Bake at 400 degrees for 15 to 20 minutes.

Fantastic Fried Corn

2 (16 ounce) packages frozen whole kernel corn
1 stick butter (not margarine)
1 cup whipping cream
1 tablespoon sugar
1 teaspoon salt

1. Place corn in a large skillet; turn on medium heat. Add the butter, whipping cream, sugar and salt.
2. Stirring constantly, heat until most of the whipping cream and butter is absorbed into the corn.

Yes, I know this corn has too many calories, but it is my grandkid's favorite vegetable and who can turn grandkids down (and actually I only fix it a couple of times a year.)

Shoe Peg Corn

1 stick margarine
1 (8 ounce) package cream cheese
3 (16 ounce) cans shoe peg corn, drained
1 (4ounce) can chopped green chilies
1 ½ cups crushed cracker crumbs

1. Melt margarine in saucepan and stir in cream cheese. Mix until cream cheese is melted.
2. Add corn and chilies (salt and pepper if you like). Mix; pour into a greased baking dish.
3. Sprinkle cracker crumbs over casserole. Bake at 350 degrees for 25 minutes.

Super Corn Casserole

1 (15 ounce) can whole kernel corn
1 (15 ounce) can cream style corn
1 stick margarine, melted
1 (8 ounce) carton sour cream
1 (6 ounce) package jalapeno cornbread mix

1. Mix all ingredients together and pour into a greased 9 x 13 inch baking dish.
2. Bake uncovered at 350 degrees for 35 minutes.
3. It is really tasty if you add ½ cup grated cheese on the top immediately after it comes out of the oven.

Corn Vegetable Medley

1 can golden corn soup
½ cup milk
2 cups fresh broccoli flowerets
2 cups cauliflower flowerets
1 cup shredded cheddar cheese

1. In saucepan over medium heat, heat soup and milk to boiling, stirring often. Stir in broccoli and cauliflowerets. Return to boiling.
2. Reduce heat to low; cover and cook 20 minutes or until vegetables are tender, stirring occasionally.
3. Stir in cheese and heat until cheese is melted.

Corn & Green Chili Casserole

2 (10 ounce) packages frozen whole kernel corn
2 tablespoons margarine
1 (8 ounce) package cream cheese
1 tablespoon sugar
1 (4 ounce) can chopped green chilies

1. Cook corn according to package directions; drain and set aside.
2. Melt margarine in saucepan over low heat; add cream cheese; stir until melted. Stir in corn, sugar and green chilies. Spoon into a greased 2 quart baking dish.
3. Cover and bake at 350 degrees for 25 minutes.

Corn and Okra Jambalaya

¼ pound bacon
1 pound fresh okra, sliced
2 onions, chopped
1 (16 ounce) can stewed tomatoes
1 (16 ounce) can whole kernel corn, drained

1. Fry bacon in large skillet until crisp, drain. In same skillet, with the bacon drippings, saute okra and onions; do not brown.
2. Add tomatoes and corn; bring to a boil. Simmer about 5 to 10 minutes. Jambalaya must not be runny.
3. Serve over hot rice. Sprinkle bacon over top of each serving.

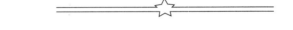

Almond Green Beans

⅓ cup slivered almonds
½ stick margarine
¾ teaspoon garlic salt
3 tablespoons lemon juice
2 (16 ounce) cans French-style green beans

1. In saucepan, cook almonds in the margarine, garlic salt and lemon juice until slightly golden brown.
2. Add drained green beans to almonds and heat.

Green Bean Revenge

3 (16 ounce) cans green beans, drained
1 (8 ounce) can sliced water chestnuts, drained,
chopped
2 (8 ounce) jars jalapeno Cheese Whiz
1 ½ cups cracker crumbs
½ stick margarine, melted

1. Place green beans in a greased 9 x 13 inch baking dish and cover with water chestnuts. Heat both jars (take lid off) of cheese in microwave just until they can be poured. Pour Cheese Whiz over green beans and water chestnuts.
2. Combine cracker crumbs and margarine; sprinkle over casserole.
3. Bake at 350 degrees for 30 minutes.

Cheesy Green Beans

¾ cup milk
1 (8 ounce) package cream cheese
½ teaspoon garlic powder
½ cup fresh parmesan cheese
2 (16 ounce) cans green beans

1. In a saucepan, combine milk, cream cheese, garlic and Parmesan cheese. Heat until cheeses are melted
2. Heat green beans in pan and drain. Cover with cream cheese mixture and toss to coat evenly. Serve hot.

Pine Nut Green Beans

1 (16 ounce) package frozen green beans
½ stick margarine
¾ cup pine nuts
¼ teaspoon garlic powder
Salt and Pepper

1. Cook beans in water in a covered 3 quart saucepan for 10 to 15 minutes or until tender-crisp; drain.
2. Melt margarine in skillet over medium heat and add pine nuts. Cook, stirring frequently until golden.
3. Add pine nuts to the green beans; add seasonings. Serve hot.

Better Butter Beans

1 cup sliced celery
1 onion, chopped
½ stick margarine
1 (10 ounce) can diced tomatoes and green chilies
2 (15 ounce) cans butter beans

1. Saute celery and onion in margarine for about 3 minutes
2. Add tomatoes and chilies, several sprinkles of salt and about ½ teaspoon sugar.
3. Add butter beans; cover and simmer about 20 minutes. Serve hot.

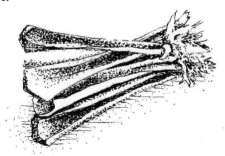

Butter Beans and Green Onions

1 (10 ounce) packages frozen butter beans
6 bacon slices, cooked, drained and crumbled
1 bunch fresh green onions, chopped
½ teaspoon garlic powder
½ cup chopped fresh parsley

1. Cook butterbeans according to package directions and set aside.
2. Saute green onions in bacon drippings. Stir in butter beans, garlic, parsley and a little salt and pepper; cook just until thoroughly heated.
3. Pour into serving bowl and sprinkle with bacon.

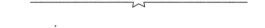

Pine Nut Broccoli

1 bunch fresh broccoli
½ stick margarine
½ cup pine nuts
⅓ cup golden raisins
2 tablespoon lemon juice

1. Steam broccoli until tender crisp. In saucepan, place margarine, nuts and raisins; saute about 3 minutes.
2. When ready to serve, add lemon juice to the nut mixture and pour over broccoli.

Broccoli Supreme

2 (10 ounce) packages broccoli spears
1 stick garlic cheese roll
1 can cream of mushroom soup
1 (3 ounce) can mushrooms, drained
¾ cup Pepperidge Farm herb dressing, crushed

1. Boil broccoli for 3 minutes and drain.
2. In saucepan, melt cheese on medium heat, in mushroom soup; add mushrooms. Combine with broccoli.
3. Pour into a 2 quart greased baking dish and top with crushed herb dressing. Bake, uncovered at 350 degrees for 30 minutes.

For a change of pace, you could use cream of chicken soup instead of the mushroom soup and leave off the mushrooms.

Heavenly Broccoli

2 (16 ounce) packages frozen broccoli spears
1 (8 ounce) container cream cheese and chives
2 cans cream of shrimp soup
2 teaspoons lemon juice
½ stick margarine, melted

1. Trim a little of the stems off broccoli and throw away. Cook broccoli in microwave as directed. Place in a 2 quart baking dish.
2. In saucepan, combine the cream cheese, soup, lemon juice and margarine. Heat just enough to mix thoroughly. Pour over broccoli.
3. Heat at 350 degrees just until hot and bubbly.

Baked Broccoli

2 (10 ounce) packages frozen broccoli spears
1 can cream of chicken soup
⅔ cup mayonnaise
¾ cup breadcrumbs
Paprika

1. Place broccoli spears in a baking dish.
2. In a saucepan, combine and heat the soup and mayonnaise; pour over broccoli. Sprinkle with breadcrumbs and paprika.
3. Bake at 325 degrees for 45 minutes.

Parmesan Broccoli

1 (16 ounce) package frozen broccoli spears
½ teaspoon garlic powder
½ cup breadcrumbs
½ stick margarine, melted
½ cup parmesan cheese

1. Cook broccoli as directed on package.
2. Drain and add garlic powder, breadcrumbs, margarine and cheese. Add salt if you like and toss.
3. Heat and serve.

Broccoli Stuffed Tomatoes

4 medium tomatoes
1 (10 ounce) package frozen chopped broccoli
1 (6 ounce) roll garlic cheese, softened
½ teaspoon garlic salt

1. Cut tops off tomatoes and scoop out pulp. Cook broccoli according to package instruction; drain well. Combine broccoli, cheese and garlic salt. Heat just until cheese is melted.
2. Stuff broccoli mixture into tomatoes and place on baking sheet.
3. Bake at 375 degrees for about 10 minutes.

Cheddar Broccoli Bake

1 can cheddar cheese soup
½ cup milk
Dash of pepper
1 (16 ounce) bag frozen broccoli flowerets, cooked
1 can French fried onion rings

1. In 2 quart casserole, mix soup, milk, pepper and broccoli.
2. Bake at 350 degrees for 25 minutes.
3. Stir. Sprinkle onions over broccoli mixture. Bake 5 more minutes or until onions are golden.

Best Cauliflower

1 (16 ounce) package frozen cauliflower
Salt and pepper
1 (8 ounce) carton sour cream
1 ½ cups grated American or cheddar cheese
4 teaspoons sesame seeds, toasted

1. Cook cauliflower as directed on package. Drain and place half of cauliflower in a 2-quart baking dish.
2. Sprinkle a little salt and pepper on cauliflower. Spread one half of the sour cream and one half of the cheese. Top with 2 teaspoons sesame seed. Repeat layers.
3. Bake at 350 degrees for about 15 to 20 minutes.

Cauliflower Medley

1 head cauliflower, cut into flowerets
1 (15 ounce) can Italian stewed tomatoes
1 bell pepper, chopped, 1 onion, chopped
½ stick margarine
1 cup shredded cheddar cheese

1. In a large saucepan, place the cauliflower, stewed tomatoes, bell pepper, onion and margarine. Add about 2 tablespoons water and some salt and pepper.
2. Cook, in the saucepan with the lid on, until the cauliflower is done, about 10 to 15 minutes. Do not let the cauliflower get mushy.
3. Place in 2 quart casserole, sprinkle cheese on top. Place in 350 degree oven just until cheese is melted.

Seasoned Squash and Onion

8 yellow squash, sliced
2 onions, chopped
½ stick margarine
1 cup grated american cheese

1. Cook squash and onion in a small amount of water until tender; drain.
2. Add margarine and cheese and toss. Serve hot.

Chile Cheese Squash

1 pound yellow squash
⅔ cup mayonnaise
1 (4 ounce) can diced green chilies, drained
⅔ cup grated longhorn cheese
⅔ cup breadcrumbs

1. Cook squash in salted water just until tender-crisp. Drain.
2. Return to saucepan, stir in mayonnaise, chilies, cheese and breadcrumbs.
3. Serve hot.

Sunny Yellow Squash

6 to 8 medium yellow squash
1 (8 ounce) package cream cheese, softened
2 tablespoons margarine
1 teaspoon sugar

1. In saucepan, cut up squash, add a little water and boil until tender. Drain
2. Add cream cheese that has been cut in chunks, margarine, sugar and a little salt and pepper.
3. Cook over low heat, stirring until cream cheese has melted.

Zucchini Patties

1 ½ cups grated zucchini
1 egg, beaten
2 tablespoons flour
⅓ cup finely minced onion
½ teaspoon seasoned salt

1. Mix all ingredients together.
2. Heat a skillet with about 3 tablespoons oil. Drop zucchini mixture by tablespoons onto the skillet at medium high heat. Turn and brown both sides.
3. Remove and drain on paper towels.

Creamed Green Peas

1 (16 ounce) package frozen English peas
¼ stick margarine
1 can cream of celery soup
1 (3 ounce) package cream cheese
1 (8 ounce) can water chestnuts, drained

1. Place peas in microwave dish and cook in microwave for 8 minutes, turning dish after 4 minutes.
2. In a large saucepan, combine margarine, soup and cream cheese. Cook on medium heat while stirring, until margarine and cream cheese have melted.
3. Add peas and water chestnuts; mix. Serve hot.

Country Baked Beans

4 (16 ounce) cans baked beans, drained
1 (12 ounce) bottle chili sauce
1 large onion, chopped
½ pound bacon, cooked and crumbled
2 cups packed brown sugar

1. In ungreased 3 quart baking dishes, combine all ingredients. Stir until blended.
2. Bake uncovered at 325 degrees for 55 minutes or until heated through.

Tasty Black-Eyed Peas

2 (10 ounce) packages frozen black-eyed peas
1 ¼ cups chopped green pepper
¾ cup chopped onion
3 tablespoons margarine
1 (15 ounce) can stewed tomatoes, undrained

1. Cook black-eyes peas according to package directions; drain.
2. Saute green pepper and onion in margarine.
3. Add peas, tomatoes and a little salt and pepper; cook over low heat until thoroughly heated, stirring often.

Fried Okra

Fresh garden okra, small size
Milk or buttermilk
Corn meal
Salt and pepper

1. Thoroughly wash and drain okra. Cut off top and ends and slice. Toss okra with a little milk or buttermilk (just enough to make the corn meal stick).
2. Sprinkle corn meal over okra and toss. Heat 2 or 3 tablespoons of oil in skillet.
3. Fry okra, turning several times until okra is golden brown and crisp.

Eggplant Fritters

1 medium size eggplant
1 egg, beaten
3 tablespoons flour
½ teaspoon salt
½ teaspoon baking powder

1. Peel and slice eggplant. Steam until tender; drain. Mash until smooth.
2. Add egg, flour, salt and baking powder, mixing well.
3. Form into patties and fry in deep hot oil.

Sauteed Celery

1 bunch celery, chopped diagonally
1 (8 ounce) can water chestnuts, drained and
   chopped
¼ cup almonds, toasted
½ stick margarine, melted

1. Boil celery in salted water just until tender crisp. Drain.
2. Saute the water chestnuts and almonds in the melted margarine..
3. Toss together the celery and the water chestnuts-almond mixture. Serve hot.

Tasty Turnips

5 medium turnips
2 teaspoons sugar
1 ½ teaspoon salt
½ stick butter (not margarine), melted

1. Peel and dice turnips. Boil with sugar and salt until tender. Drain.
2. Add butter to turnips and mash. Serve hot.

Sour Cream Cabbage

1 medium head cabbage, cooked tender crisp, drained
2 tablespoons margarine
1 tablespoon sugar, ¼ teaspoon nutmeg
1 (4 ounce) jar pimentos, drained
1 (8 ounce) package cream cheese

1. Combine cabbage, margarine, sugar, nutmeg and pimentos in saucepan.
2. Cook until cabbage is tender-crisp. (But don't overcook.)
3. Add cream cheese while on low heat. Stir until cream cheese has melted.

Spicy Hominy

1 (16 ounce) can yellow hominy, drained
1 (8 ounce) carton sour cream
1 (4 ounce) can chopped green chiles
1 ¼ cups grated cheddar cheese

1. Combine all ingredients, adding a little salt.
2. Pour into a one quart baking dish and bake at 350 degrees for about 20 minutes.

Creamed Spinach Bake

2 (10 ounce) packages frozen chopped spinach
2 (3 ounce) packages cream cheese, softened
3 tablespoons margarine
1 cup seasoned breadcrumbs

1. Cook spinach according to package directions and drain. Combine cream cheese and margarine with the spinach; heat until cream cheese and margarine are melted and mixed well with the spinach. Pour into a greased baking dish.
2. Sprinkle a little salt over spinach; then cover with the breadcrumbs.
3. Bake at 350 degrees for 15 to 20 minutes.

Spinach Casserole

1 (16 ounce) package frozen chopped spinach
1 (8 ounce) package cream cheese and chives
1 can cream of mushroom soup
1 egg, beaten
Cracker crumbs

1. Cook spinach according to directions; drain. Blend cream cheese and soup with egg.
2. Mix with spinach and pour into a buttered casserole. Top with cracker crumbs.
3. Bake at 350 degrees for 35 minutes.

Cheese Please Spinach

1 (16 ounce) package frozen chopped spinach
3 eggs
½ cup flour
1 (16 ounce) carton small curd cottage cheese
2 cups shredded cheddar cheese

1. Cook spinach, drain and set aside. Beat eggs; add flour, cottage cheese and a little salt and pepper. Stir in spinach and cheddar cheese. Pour into a 1 ½ quart baking dish.
2. Bake uncovered at 350 degrees for 35 minutes.

Green Rice and Spinach

1 cup uncooked rice, (use instant)
1 (10 ounce) package frozen chopped spinach
1 onion, finely chopped
3 tablespoons margarine
¾ cup grated cheddar cheese

1. Cook rice in a large saucepan. Punch holes in box of spinach and cook in microwave about 3 minutes.
2. Reserve 3 tablespoons cheese for topping. Add spinach, onion, margarine, cheese, rice and ¼ teaspoon salt. If it seems a little dry, add a couple tablespoons of water. Pour into a 2 quart greased baking dish.
3. Bake at 350 degrees for 25 minutes.

Baked Tomatoes

2 (16 ounce) cans diced tomatoes, drained
1 ½ cups toasted breadcrumbs, divided
A scant ¼ cup sugar
½ onion, chopped
4 tablespoons margarine, melted

1. Combine the tomatoes, 1 cup of the breadcrumbs, sugar, onion and margarine.
2. Pour into a buttered baking dish and cover with remaining breadcrumbs.
3. Bake at 325 degrees for 25 to 30 minutes or until crumbs are lightly brown.

Okra Gumbo

1 large onion, chopped
1 pound fresh okra, cut in slices
4 tablespoons margarine
2 (15 ounce) cans tomatoes
1 potato, chopped

1. Brown onion and okra in the margarine.
2. Add the tomatoes and potato; bring to a boil.
3. Simmer until potatoes are done, about 30 minutes.

Cheesy Vegetable Sauce

½ cup shredded cheddar cheese
½ cup sour cream
½ stick margarine
2 tablespoons chopped fresh parsley
½ teaspoon garlic powder

1. Combine all ingredients in a 3 quart glass bowl. Micro-wave at MEDIUM-HIGH for 2 minutes or until cheese melts, stirring at 1 minute intervals with a wire whisk.
2. Serve over cooked broccoli, cauliflower or even potatoes.

Mixed Vegetable and Cheese Casserole

1 (16 ounce) packages frozen mixed vegetables
1 ¾ cup shredded American cheese
¾ cup mayonnaise
1 tube Ritz crackers, crushed
¾ stick margarine, melted

1. Cook vegetables according to directions; drain. Place in a 2 quart buttered casserole dish.
2. Mix cheese and mayonnaise and spread over vegetables. Mix cracker crumbs and margarine and sprinkle on top .
3. Bake at 350 degrees for 35 minutes.

These vegetables are worthy of Sunday dinner and besides that, this is the way to get the kids to eat vegetables.

Herb Seasoned Vegetables

1 (14 ounce) can seasoned chicken broth with Italian herbs
½ teaspoon garlic powder
1 (16 ounce) package frozen vegetables (broccoli, cauliflower, etc.)
¼ cup grated parmesan cheese

1. Heat broth, garlic and vegetables; heat to a boil.
2. Cover and cook over low heat for 5 minutes or until tender-crisp. Drain.
3. Place in serving dish and sprinkle cheese over vegetables.

Creamy Vegetable Casserole

**1 (16 ounce) package frozen broccoli, carrots and
   cauliflower**
1 can cream of mushroom soup, undiluted
**1 (8 ounce) carton spreadable garden vegetable
   cream cheese**
1 cup seasoned croutons

1. Cook vegetables according to package directions; drain
   and place in a large bowl.
2. In a saucepan, place the soup and cream cheese, heat just
   enough to mix easily. Pour into the vegetable mixture,
   mixing well. Pour into a 2 quart baking dish. Sprinkle
   with croutons.
3. Bake uncovered at 375 degrees for 25 minutes or until
   bubbly.

Baked Beans

2 (15 ounce) cans pork and beans, slightly drained
½ onion, finely chopped
⅔ cup brown sugar
¼ cup chili sauce
1 tablespoon Worcestershire
2 strips bacon

1. In bowl, combine beans, onion, brown sugar, chili sauce
   and Worcestershire.
2. Pour into a buttered 2 quart casserole dish and place
   bacon strips over beans.
3. Bake uncovered at 325 degrees for 50 minutes.

Zucchini au Gratin

6 medium zucchini, sliced
1 onion, chopped
1 (8 ounce) carton sour cream
1 ¼ cups grated cheddar cheese
2 teaspoons toasted sesame seeds

1. Cook zucchini and onion in a little salted water. Do not over cook. Drain well.
2. Place half the zucchini mixture in a buttered 2 quart casserole; sprinkle with salt and pepper. Spread with half the sour cream and half the cheese. Repeat layer.
3. Top with sesame seeds. Bake, uncovered at 350 degrees about 15 minutes.

Zucchini Bake

4 cups grated zucchini
1 ½ cups grated Monterey Jack cheese
4 eggs, beaten
2 cups cheese crackers crumbs

1. In a bowl, combine zucchini, cheese and eggs, mixing well.
2. Spoon into a buttered 3 quart baking dish. Sprinkle crackers crumbs over top.
3. Bake uncovered at 350 degrees for 35 minutes.

Mashed Potatoes Supreme

1 (8 ounce) package cream cheese, softened
½ cup sour cream
¼ stick margarine, softened
1 envelope ranch salad dressing mix
6 to 8 cups warm mashed potatoes (use instant)

1. With mixer, combine cream cheese, sour cream, margarine and salad dressing, mixing well. Add potatoes, stirring well.
2. Transfer to a 2 quart casserole dish.
3. Bake at 350 degrees for 25 minutes or until heated through and through.

Creamy Mashed Potatoes

6 large potatoes
1 (8 ounce) carton sour cream
1 (8 ounce) package cream cheese, softened
1 teaspoon salt
½ teaspoon white pepper

1. Peel, cut up and boil the potatoes. Drain. Add sour cream, cream cheese, salt and pepper. Whip until cream cheese has melted. Pour into greased 3 quart baking dish.
2. Cover with foil and bake at 325 degrees for about 20 minutes. (About 10 minutes longer if you are reheating them.)

Ranch Mashed Potatoes

**4 cups prepared, unsalted mashed potatoes (use
     instant)
1 packet Hidden Valley Ranch dressing mix
½ stick margarine**

1. Combine all ingredients in saucepan. Heat on low until
   potatoes are thoroughly heated.

Loaded Baked Potatoes

**6 medium to large potatoes
1 (1 pound) hot sausage
1 (2 pound) box Velveeta cheese
1 (10 ounce) can Rotel tomatoes and green chilies**

1. Wrap potatoes in foil and bake at 375 degrees for 1 hour
   or until done.
2. Brown sausage and drain. Cut cheese into chunks and
   add to sausage. Heat until cheese is melted; add the
   tomatoes and green chilies.
3. Serve the sausage-cheese mixture over baked potatoes.

Broccoli Cheese Potato Topper

1 (10 ounce) can Fiesta Nacho cheese (with the soups)
2 tablespoons sour cream
½ teaspoon Dijon mustard
1 (10 ounce) box frozen broccoli flowerets, cooked
4 medium potatoes, baked and fluffed

1. In 1 quart microwave-safe casserole, stir soup, sour cream, mustard and broccoli. Heat in microwave 2 to 2 ½ minutes.
2. Spoon over split potatoes.

Scalloped Potatoes

6 medium potatoes
1 stick margarine
1 tablespoon flour
2 cups grated cheddar cheese
¾ cup milk

1. Peel and slice half of the potatoes and place in a 3 quart greased baking dish. Slice half the margarine over potatoes. Sprinkle flour over potatoes. Cover with half the cheese.
2. Repeat layers with cheese on top. Pour milk over casserole and sprinkle on a little pepper. Prepare the potatoes as fast as you can so they will not turn dark.
3. Cover and bake at 350 degrees for one hour.

Potatoes Au Gratin

½ pound Velveeta cheese
1 pint half and half
1 cup shredded cheddar cheese
1 stick margarine
1 (2 pound) package frozen hash brown potatoes

1. In double boiler, melt first 4 ingredients. Place hash brown in a greased 9 x 13 inch baking dish. Pour cheese mixture over potatoes.
2. Bake, uncovered at 350 degrees for 1 hour.

Twice-Baked Potatoes

8 medium baking potatoes
¼ stick margarine
½ teaspoon salt
1 can cheddar cheese soup
1 tablespoon chopped dried chives

1. Bake potatoes until done. Cut potatoes in half lengthwise; scoop out insides leaving a thin shell. With mixer, whip potatoes with margarine and salt.
2. Gradually add soup and chives; beat until light and fluffy. (If you want a little "zip" to the potatoes us a 10 ounce can of Fiesta Nacho Cheese instead of the cheese soup).
3. Spoon into shells. Sprinkle with paprika. Bake at 425 degrees for 15 minutes.

Chive Potato Souffle

3 eggs, separated
2 cups hot mashed potatoes (use instant)
½ cup sour cream
2 heaping tablespoons chopped chives
1 teaspoon seasoned salt

1. Beat egg whites until stiff. Set aside. Beat yolks until smooth and add to potatoes.
2. Fold in beaten egg whites, sour cream, chives and salt. Pour into a buttered 2 quart baking dish.
3. Bake at 350 degrees for 45 minutes.

Cheddar Potato Strips

3 large potatoes, cut into ½ inch strips
½ cup milk
2 tablespoons margarine
½ cup shredded cheddar cheese
1 tablespoon minced fresh parsley

1. In a greased 9 x 13 inch baking dish, arrange potatoes in a single layer. Pour milk over potatoes. Dot with margarine and sprinkle a little salt and pepper.
2. Cover and bake at 400 degrees for 30 minutes or until potatoes are tender.
3. Sprinkle with cheese and parsley. Bake, uncovered 5 minutes longer.

Oven Fries

5 medium baking potatoes
⅓ cup oil
¼ teaspoon black pepper
¾ seasoned salt
Paprika

1. Scrub potatoes and cut each in 6 lengthwise wedges. Place potatoes in a shallow baking dish. Combine oil, pepper and seasoned salt; brush potatoes with this mixture.
2. Sprinkle lightly with paprika. Bake at 375 degrees for about 50 minutes or until potatoes are tender and lightly browned.
3. Baste twice with remaining oil mixture while baking.

Terrific 'Taters

5 to 6 medium potatoes
1 (8 ounce) carton sour cream
1 package Ranch Salad dressing mix (dry)
1 ½ cups shredded cheddar cheese
3 pieces bacon, fried, drained and crumbled

1. Peel, slice and boil potatoes; drain. Place potatoes in a 2 quart baking dish.
2. Combine sour cream, salad dressing mix and a little pepper. Toss until potatoes are coated. Sprinkle cheese on top.
3. Bake at 350 degrees for about 20 minutes. Sprinkle bacon on top. Serve hot.

Herbed New Potatoes

1 ½ pounds new potatoes
¾ stick butter, cut into slices
¼ teaspoon thyme
½ cup chopped fresh parsley
½ teaspoon rosemary

1. Scrub potatoes and cut in halves; do not peel. In medium saucepan, boil in lightly salted water. Cook until potatoes are tender, about 20 minutes. Drain.
2. Add butter, thyme, parsley and rosemary. Toss gently until butter is melted.
3. Serve hot.

Carnival Couscous

1 (5.7 ounce) box herbed chicken couscous
½ stick margarine
1 red bell pepper, cut in tiny pieces
1 yellow squash, cut in tiny pieces (cut out inside seeds)
¾ cup fresh broccoli flowerets, finely chopped

1. Cook couscous as package directs, leaving out the butter.
2. With margarine in saucepan, saute the bell pepper, squash and broccoli; cooking about 10 minutes or until vegetables are almost tender.
3. Combine couscous and vegetables. (If you want to do this a little ahead of time, place couscous and vegetable in a Pam sprayed baking dish. Heat in a 325 degrees oven for about 20 minutes).

This is a delicious and colorful dish – a recipe that takes the place of rice and a vegetable.

Macaroni, Cheese and Tomatoes

2 cups elbow macaroni, uncooked
1 (14 ounce) can stewed tomatoes, undrained
1 (8 ounce) package shredded cheddar cheese
2 tablespoons sugar
1 (6 ounce) package cheese slices

1. Cook macaroni according to directions; drain. In large bowl, combine macaroni tomatoes, shredded cheese, sugar, ¼ cup water and a little salt. Mix well.
2. Pour into a 9 x 13 inch baking dish and place cheese slices on top.
3. Bake at 350 degrees for 30 minutes or until bubbly.

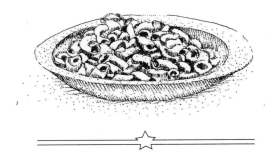

Red Rice

1 (16 ounce) package smoked sausage, sliced
2 (10 ounce) cans diced tomato and green chiles
3 cups chicken broth
2 teaspoons Creole seasoning
1 ½ cups uncooked long-grain rice

1. Saute sausage in Dutch oven until browned. Stir in tomato and green chiles, broth and seasoning; bring to a boil.
2. Stir in rice; cover, reduce heat and simmer 25 minutes.
3. Uncover and cook until liquid is absorbed.

Green Chili-Rice

1 cup rice, cooked (use instant)
1 (12 ounce) package shredded Monterrey Jack cheese
1 (7 ounce) can chopped green chilies
2 (8 ounce) cartons sour cream
½ teaspoon garlic powder

1. In large bowl, combine and mix all ingredients; adding a little salt if you like.
2. Spoon into a greased 9 x 13 inch baking dish and bake covered at 350 degrees for 30 minutes.

Grits Souffle

1 ½ cups grits
1 ½ teaspoon salt
1 stick margarine
1 ½ cups shredded cheddar cheese
5 eggs, beaten

1. Boil grits in 6 cups salted water. Stir in margarine and cheese, stirring until cheese is melted. Allow to cool until lukewarm.
2. Add eggs and pour into a greased 2 quart baking dish.
3. Bake covered at 350 degrees for 45 minutes.

Favorite Pasta

4 ounces spinach linguine, uncooked
1 cup whipping cream
1 cup chicken broth
½ cup freshly grated parmesan cheese
½ cup frozen English peas

1. Cook linguine according to package directions; drain and keep warm
2. Combine whipping cream and chicken broth in a saucepan; bring to a boil. Reduce heat and simmer 25 minutes or until thickened and reduced to 1 cup. Remove from heat.
3. Add cheese and peas, stirring until cheese melts. Toss with linguine and serve immediately.

Pasta With Basil

2 ½ cups uncooked small tube pasta
1 small onion, chopped
2 tablespoons oil
2 ½ tablespoons dried basil
1 cup shredded mozzarella cheese

1. Cook pasta according to package directions. In a skillet, saute onion in oil.
2. Stir in basil and 1 teaspoon salt and ¼ teaspoon pepper; cook and stir 1 minute. Drain pasta leaving about ½ cup so the pasta won't be too dry and add to basil mixture.
3. Remove from heat, stir in cheese just until it begins to melt. Serve immediately.

Creamy Seasoned Noodles

1 (8 ounce) package wide egg noodles
1 envelope Good Seasons's Italian salad dressing
   mix
½ cup whipping cream
½ stick margarine
¼ cup grated parmesan cheese

1. Cook noodles as directed on package; drain.
2. Add remaining ingredients (cut margarine in chunks so it will melt easier) and toss lightly to blend thoroughly.
3. Serve hot.

Sweet Potato Wedges

3 pounds sweet potatoes, peeled and quartered
   lengthwise
6 tablespoons margarine, melted
6 tablespoons orange juice
¾ teaspoon salt
¾ teaspoon ground cinnamon

1. Arrange sweet potatoes in a greased 9 x 13 inch baking pan. Combine the margarine, orange juice, salt and cinnamon; drizzle over sweet potatoes.
2. Cover and bake at 350 degrees for 60 minutes or until tender.

Speedy Sweet Potatoes

2 (16 ounce) cans sweet potatoes, drained
1 (8 ounce) can crushed pineapple, undrained
½ cup chopped pecans
⅓ cup packed brown sugar
1 cup miniature marshmallows

1. In a 2 quart microwave-safe dish, layer sweet potatoes, a little salt, pineapple, pecans, brown sugar and ½ cup marshmallows. Cover and microwave on high for 6 minutes or until bubbly around the edges.
2. Top with remaining marshmallows. Heat uncovered on high for 30 seconds or until marshmallows puff. If you like, sprinkle sweet potatoes with a little nutmeg.

Festive Cranberry Stuffing

1 (14 ounce) can chicken broth
1 rib celery, chopped
½ cup fresh or frozen cranberries
1 small onion, chopped
4 cups Pepperidge Farm herb seasoned stuffing

1. Mix broth, a dash of black pepper, celery, cranberries and onion in saucepan. Heat to a boil. Cover and cook over low heat 5 minutes .
2. Add stuffing and mix lightly.
3. Place in 325 degree oven just until thoroughly heated.

Hopping John

**2 (16 ounce) cans Jalapena black-eyed peas,
  undrained
¾ pound ham, chopped
1 cup chopped onion
2 cups hot cooked rice
½ cup chopped green onions**

1. In a saucepan, combing peas, ham and onion.   Bring to a boil, reduce heat and simmer 15 minutes.
2. Stir in hot rice and green onions. Serve hot.

Maple-Ginger Sweet Potatoes

**4 medium-size sweet potatoes
½ cup sour cream
2 tablespoons maple syrup
¼ teaspoon ground ginger
¼ cup chopped pecans**

1. Pierce sweet potatoes several times with fork and place on a baking sheet. Bake at 375 degrees for 1 hour.
2. Stir together sour cream and next 2 ingredients. Spoon over split potatoes and sprinkle with pecans.

Notes

MAIN DISHES

Chicken Ole

6 chicken breasts, boned and skinned
1 (8 ounce) package cream cheese, softened
1 (16 ounce) jar picante sauce
2 teaspoons cumin
1 cup fresh green onion, chopped, tops too

1. Pound chicken breasts to flatten. In mixer beat cream cheese until smooth; add picante, cumin and onions. Place a heaping spoonful of mixture on each chicken breast and roll. Place seam side down, in shallow baking pan.
2. Pour remaining sauce over top of chicken rolls.
3. Bake uncovered at 350 degrees for 50 minutes.

Great Served With:
Easy Guacamole Salad • Shoe Peg Corn

Chicken Crunch

4 chicken breast halves, skinned and boned
½ cup Italian salad dressing
½ cup sour cream
2 ½ cups cornflakes, crushed

1. Place chicken in a zip-top plastic bag; add salad dressing and sour cream. Seal, refrigerate 1 hour. Remove chicken from marinade , discarding marinade.
2. Dredge chicken in cornflakes; place in a 9 x 13 inch Pam sprayed baking dish.
3. Bake at 375 degrees for 45 minutes.

Great Served With:
Baked Broccoli • Mediterranean Potato Salad

Favorite Chicken Breasts

6 to 8 chicken breasts, skinned and boned
1 can cream of mushroom soup
¾ cup white wine (or white cooking wine)
1 (8 ounce) carton sour cream

1. Place chicken breasts in a large, shallow baking pan. Sprinkle on a little salt and pepper. Bake uncovered at 350 degrees for 30 minutes.
2. In saucepan, combine soup, wine and sour cream; heat just enough to mix together. Remove chicken from oven and pour sour cream mixture over chicken.
3. Return to oven to cook another 30 minutes. Baste twice again. Serve over rice.

Great Served With:
Broccoli-Cauliflower Salad • Corn and Green Chili Casserole

Broccoli Cheese Chicken

1 tablespoon margarine
4 chicken breast, skinned and boned
1 can condensed broccoli cheese soup
1 (10 ounce) package frozen broccoli spears
⅓ cup milk

1. In skillet, heat margarine and cook chicken 15 minutes, until brown on both sides. Remove, set aside.
2. In same skillet, combine soup, broccoli, milk and a little black pepper. Heat to boiling. Return chicken to skillet. Reduce heat to low.
3. Cover and cook another 25 minutes until chicken is no longer pink and broccoli is tender. Serve over rice.

Great Served With:
Pine Nut Green Beans • Marinated Cucumbers

Hawaiian Chicken

2 small size chickens, cut in quarters
Flour to coat chicken
Oil
1 (20 ounce) can sliced pineapple, reserving juice
2 bell peppers, cut in strips

1. Pat chicken dry with paper towels. Coat chicken with salt, pepper and flour. Brown chicken in the oil and place in a shallow pan.
2. Drain pineapple, pouring syrup into a 2 cup measure. Add water (or orange juice if you have it) to make 1 ½ cups liquid. Reserve juice for sauce.

Sauce for Hawaiian Chicken

1 cup sugar
3 tablespoons cornstarch
¾ cup vinegar, 1 tablespoon lemon juice
1 tablespoon soy sauce
2 teaspoons chicken bouillon

1. In medium saucepan, combine the 1 ½ cups of juice, the sugar, cornstarch, vinegar, lemon juice, soy sauce and chicken bouillon. Bring to a boil, stirring constantly until thickened and clear. Pour over chicken. Bake at 350 degrees, covered for 40 minutes.
2. Place pineapple slices and bell pepper on top of chicken and bake another 10 minutes. Serve on fluffy white rice.

Great Served With:
Butter Mint Salad • Asparagus Bake

Apricot Chicken

1 cup apricot preserves
1 (8 ounce) bottle Catalina dressing
1 package onion soup mix
6 to 8 chicken breasts

1. In a bowl, mix apricot preserves, dressing and soup mix. Place chicken breasts in a large, buttered baking dish and pour apricot mixture over chicken. (For a change of pace, use Russian dressing instead of Catalina).
2. Bake uncovered at 325 degrees for 1 hour and 20 minutes. Serve over hot rice.

Great Served With:
Asparagus Bake • Nutty Green Salad

Pineapple Teriyaki Chicken

6 chicken breasts, skinned and boned
½ red onion, sliced
1 green bell pepper, cored, seeded and sliced
1 cup Lawry's Teriyaki marinade with pineapple juice, divided
1 (15 ounce) can pineapple rings, drained

1. Spray a 9 x 13 inch baking dish and place chicken in dish. Arrange vegetables over chicken.
2. Pour marinade over vegetables and chicken.
3. Bake uncovered at 350 degrees for 45 minutes. Spoon juices over chicken once during baking. About 10 minutes before chicken is done, place pineapple slices over chicken and return to oven.

Great Served With:
Broccoli Waldorf Salad • Asparagus Caesar

Hurry-Up Chicken Enchiladas

2 ½ to 3 cups chicken breast, cooked and cubed
1 can cream of chicken soup
1 ½ cups chunky salsa
8 (6 inch) flour tortillas
1 can Fiesta Nacho cheese (found with the soups)

1. In saucepan, combine chicken, soup and ½ cup salsa. Heat through.
2. Spoon about ⅓ cup chicken mixture down center of each tortilla. Roll up tortilla around filling and place, seam-side down in a Pam sprayed 9 x 13 inch baking dish.
3. Mix Nacho cheese, remaining salsa and ¼ cup water; pour over enchiladas. Cover with waxed paper and microwave on high, turning several times, for 5 minutes or until bubbly.

Great Served With:
Green Bean Revenge • Easy Guacamole Salad

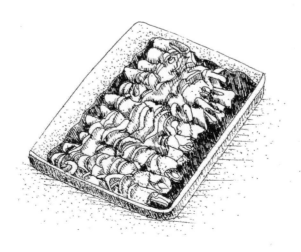

Dijon Chicken in a Skillet

¼ cup prepared ranch salad dressing
1 tablespoon Dijon mustard
4 chicken breast halves, skinned and boned
2 tablespoons margarine
3 tablespoons white wine or chicken broth

1. In bowl, combine salad dressing and mustard; set aside. In a skillet, cook chicken in margarine; let simmer for 10 to 15 minutes.
2. Add wine or broth and simmer another 20 minutes.
3. Whisk in mustard mixture; cook and stir until blended and heated through. Serve over instant long grain and wild rice.

Great Served With:
Super Corn Casserole • Broccoli Noodle Salad

Chicken Marseilles

3 tablespoons margarine
5 to 6 chicken breast halves, skinned and boned
1 package Knorr vegetable soup and dip mix
½ teaspoon dillweed
½ cup sour cream

1. Melt margarine in skillet and brown chicken, turning occasionally about 10 to 15 minutes.
2. Stir into skillet 2 cups water, soup mix and dill; bring to a boil. Reduce heat; cover and simmer, stirring occasionally, for 25 to 30 minutes or until chicken is tender. You will want to serve this delicious chicken over brown rice (use instant). Have your rice cooked and ready when chicken has cooked. Remove chicken to a heated plate.
3. After removing chicken and the heat is still on under the skillet, stir in sour cream, stirring until creamy. Place rice on individual plates or a large platter. Lay chicken breasts over rice and spoon sauce over chicken and rice.

This is a simple, but elegant dinner entrée. It is not only pleasing to the eye with the colorful vegetables from the soup mix, you will think you're in France with this bountiful sauce.

Great Served With:
Summertime Mushroom Salad • Nutty Green Salad

Baked Chicken Poupon

2 tablespoons Grey Poupon Dijon mustard
2 tablespoons oil
1 teaspoon garlic powder
½ teaspoon Italian seasoning
4 chicken breasts halves, boned and skinned

1. Mix Grey Poupon Dijon mustard, oil, garlic powder and seasoning in a plastic bag. Add chicken breasts and let set for 15 minutes.
2. Place chicken in a Pam sprayed shallow baking pan.
3. Bake uncovered at 375 degrees for 35 minutes.

Great Served With:
Broccoli Cheese Potato Topper
Cottage Cheese and Fruit Salad

Grilled Chicken Cordon Bleu

6 chicken breast halves, skinned and boned
6 slices Swiss cheese
6 thin slices deli ham
3 tablespoons oil
1 cup seasoned breadcrumbs

1. Flatten chicken to ¼ inch thickness. Place a slice of cheese and ham on each to within ¼ inch of edges. Fold in half; secure with toothpicks. Brush with oil and roll in breadcrumbs.
2. Grill, covered, over medium – hot heat for 15 to 18 minutes or until juices run clear.

Great Served With:
Mediterranean Potato Salad • Marinated Brussel Sprouts

Chicken Cutlets

6 chicken breasts, skinned and boned
1 ½ cups dry breadcrumbs
½ cup grated parmesan cheese
1 teaspoon dried basil
½ teaspoon garlic powder
1 (8 ounce) carton sour cream

1. Flatten chicken to ½ inch thickness. In a shallow dish, combine the breadcrumbs, parmesan cheese, basil and garlic powder.
2. Dip chicken in sour cream, then coat with the crumb mixture. Place in a 10 x 15 inch (so chicken breasts do not touch) greased baking dish.
3. Bake uncovered at 325 degrees for 50 to 60 minutes or until golden brown.

Great Served With:
Carnival Couscous • Pistachio Salad

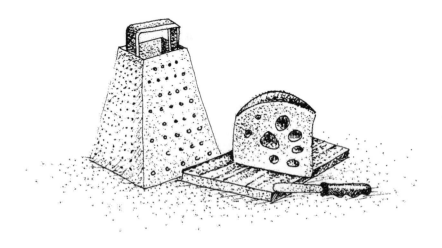

Asparagus Cheese Chicken

1 tablespoon margarine
4 chicken breast, skinned and boned
1 can condensed broccoli cheese soup
1 (10 ounce) package frozen asparagus cuts
⅓ cup milk

1. In a skillet, heat margarine and cook chicken 10 to 15 minutes, until brown on both sides. Remove chicken, set aside.
2. In same skillet, combine soup, asparagus, and milk. Heat to boiling. Return chicken to skillet. Reduce heat to low.
3. Cover and cook another 25 minutes until chicken is no longer pink and asparagus is tender.

Great Served With:
Cream Cheese and Mango Salad • Shoe Peg Corn

One Dish Chicken Bake

1 (6 ounce) package chicken stuffing mix
1 ⅔ cup water
4 chicken breasts halves, skinned
1 can cream of mushroom soup
⅓ cup sour cream

1. Toss contents of vegetable-seasoning packet, stuffing mix and water; set aside.
2. Place chicken in a greased 9 x 13 inch baking dish. Mix soup and sour cream in saucepan over how heat – just enough to pour. Pour over chicken. Spoon stuffing evenly over top.
3. Bake uncovered at 375 degrees for 40 minutes.

Great Served With:
Garlic Green Beans • Luscious Strawberry Salad

Tangy Chicken

1 (2 pound) broiler-fryer chicken, cut up
3 tablespoons margarine
½ cup Heinz 57 sauce
½ cup water

1. Brown chicken pieces in skillet with the margarine. Place chicken pieces in shallow pan.
2. Combine sauce and water; pour over chicken. Cover with foil.
3. Bake at 350 degrees for 45 minutes. Remove foil last 10 minutes of cooking time so chicken can brown.

Great Served With:
Creamy Mashed Potatoes • Broccoli-Cauliflower Salad

Curry Glazed Chicken

3 tablespoons margarine
⅓ cup honey
2 tablespoons Dijon prepared mustard
1 ½ teaspoon curry powder
4 chicken breasts, skinned and boned

1. Place margarine in 9x 13 inch baking pan; heat oven to 375 degrees to melt the margarine.
2. Mix honey, mustard and curry powder in pan with the margarine. Add chicken to pan, turning mixture until chicken is coated.
3. Bake uncovered for 50 minutes and basting twice. Serve over rice.

Great Served With:
Broccoli Waldorf Salad • Corn Vegetable Medley

Honey Baked Chicken

2 chickens, cut in quarters
1 stick margarine, melted
⅔ cup honey
¼ cup Dijon mustard
1 teaspoon curry powder

1. Place chicken pieces in a large shallow baking dish, skin side up; sprinkle a little salt over chicken.
2. Combine margarine, honey, mustard and curry powder.
3. Pour over chicken and bake uncovered at 350 degrees for 1 hour and 15 minutes; basting every 20 minutes.

Great Served With:
Broccoli Supreme • Sunflower Salad

Sweet and Sour Chicken

6 to 8 chicken breasts, skinned and boned
Oil
1 package onion soup mix (dry)
1 (6 ounce) can frozen orange juice concentrate, thawed
⅔ cup water

1. Brown chicken in a little oil or margarine. Place chicken in a greased 9 x 13 inch baking dish.
2. In small bowl, combine onion soup mix, orange juice and water, mixing well. Pour over chicken.
3. Bake uncovered at 350 degrees, for 45 to 50 minutes.

Great Served With:
Mixed Vegetables and Cheese • Divinity Salad

Bacon-Wrapped Chicken

6 chicken breast halves, skinned and boned
1 (8 ounce) carton whipped cream cheese with
onion and chives
Margarine
6 bacon strips

1. Flatten chicken to ½ inch thickness. Spread 3 tablespoons cream cheese over each. Dot with margarine and a little salt. Roll up. Wrap each with a bacon strip. Place seam side down in a greased 9 x 13 inch baking dish.
2. Bake, uncovered at 375 degrees for 40 to 45 minutes or until juices run clear.
3. To brown, broil 6 inches from heat for about 3 minutes or until bacon is crisp.

Great Served With:
Creamed Green Peas • Spinach Rice Salad

Oregano Chicken

½ stick margarine, melted
1 envelope Italian salad dressing mix
2 tablespoons lemon juice
4 chicken breast halves, skinned and boned
2 tablespoons dried oregano

1. Combine margarine, salad dressing mix and lemon juice. Place chicken in an ungreased 9 x 13 inch baking pan. Spoon margarine mixture over chicken.
2. Cover and bake at 350 degrees for 45 minutes. Uncover and baste with pan drippings and sprinkle with oregano.
3. Bake another 15 minutes longer or until chicken juices run clear.

Great Served With:
Winter Salad • Green Rice and Spinach

Oven-Fried Chicken

⅔ cup fine, dry breadcrumbs
⅓ cup grated parmesan cheese
½ teaspoon garlic salt
6 chicken breast halves, skinned and boned
¼ cup Italian salad dressing

1. In small bowl, combine breadcrumbs, cheese and garlic salt. Dip chicken in salad dressing, then dredge in crumb mixture. Place chicken in a 9 x 13 inch Pam sprayed pan.
2. Bake uncovered at 350 degrees for 50 minutes.

Great Served With:
Baked Tomatoes • Spinach and Apple Salad

Party Chicken Breasts

6 to 8 chicken breasts, skinned and boned
8 strips bacon
1 (1.5 ounce) jar chipped beef
1 can cream of chicken soup
1 (8 ounce) carton sour cream

1. Wrap each chicken breast with a strip of bacon and secure with toothpicks. Place chipped beef in bottom of a large, shallow baking pan. Top with chicken.
2. Heat soup and sour cream, just enough for it to be poured over chicken.
3. Bake uncovered in a 325 degree oven for one hour.

Great Served With:
Almond Green Beans • Terrific Tortellini Salad

Fruited Chicken

6 large chicken breasts, skinned and boned
1 stick margarine, melted
⅔ cup flour
1 (15 ounce) can chunky fruit cocktail, drained but
keeping juice
Salt, pepper and paprika

1. Dip chicken in margarine and then in flour. Place in a 9 x 13 inch shallow baking dish. Sprinkle with a little salt, pepper and paprika.
2. Bake, uncovered at 350 degrees for 45 minutes.
3. Uncover and pour fruit and half of juice over chicken. Bake another 20 minutes.

Great Served With:
Special Rice Salad • Corn Vegetable Medley

Picante Chicken

4 chicken breasts, boned and skinned
1 (16 ounce) jar picante sauce
4 tablespoons brown sugar
1 tablespoon prepared mustard
Hot cooked rice

1. Place chicken in a Pam sprayed shallow baking dish.
2. In a small bowl, combine picante sauce, brown sugar and mustard; pour over chicken.
3. Bake uncovered at 375 degrees for 45 minutes or until chicken juices run clear. Serve over rice.

Great Served With:
City Slicker Salad • Corn and Green Chili Casserole

Ranch Chicken

2 pounds chicken drumsticks (8 or 9)
1 stick margarine, melted
½ cup parmesan cheese
1 ½ cups cornflakes
1 package Hidden Valley Ranch dressing mix (dry)

1. Dip washed and dried chicken in melted margarine. Combine cheese, cornflakes and dressing mix. Dredge chicken in this mixture.
2. Bake uncovered at 350 degrees for 50 minutes or until golden.

Great Served With:
Scalloped Potatoes • Broccoli Noodle Salad

Cranberry Chicken

6 chicken breasts halves, skinned and boned
1 (16 ounce) can whole berry cranberry sauce
1 large tart apple, peeled and chopped
⅓ cup chopped walnuts
1 teaspoon curry powder

1. Place chicken in a Pam sprayed 9 x 13 inch baking pan. Bake uncovered at 350 degrees for 20 minutes.
2. Combine the remaining ingredients and spoon over chicken.
3. Bake uncovered 25 minutes longer or until chicken juices run clear.

Great Served With:
Garlic Green Beans • Marinated Corn Salad

Roasted Chicken and Vegetables

3 pounds chicken parts
1 cup Lawry's lemon pepper marinade with lemon juice, divided
1 (16 ounce) package frozen mixed vegetables, thawed
¼ cup olive oil
1 tablespoon seasoned salt

1. Spray baking pan with Pam. Arrange chicken skin-side down in pan. Pour ⅔ cup marinade over chicken. Bake uncovered at 375 degrees for 30 minutes.
2. Turn chicken over and baste with remaining ⅓ cup marinade.
3. Open the package of vegetables and toss with the oil and seasoned salt. Arrange vegetables around chicken and cover with foil; return pan to oven and bake another 30 minutes.

Great Served With:
Herbed New Potatoes • Frozen Cherry Salad

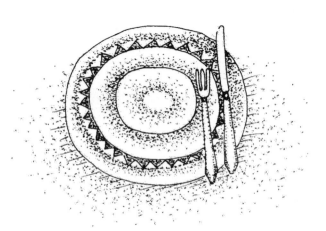

Maple-Plum Glazed Turkey Breast

2 cup red plum jam
1 cup maple syrup
1 teaspoon dry mustard
¼ cup lemon juice
1 (5 pound) bone-in turkey breast

1. In saucepan, combine first 4 ingredients. Bring to boiling point, turn heat down and simmer for about 20 minutes or until thickened. Reserve 1 cup.
2. Place turkey breast in roaster and pour remaining glaze over turkey. Bake according to directions on the turkey breast.
3. Slice turkey and serve with heated reserved glaze.

Great Served With:
Frozen Cranberry-Pineapple Salad • Cheesy Green Beans

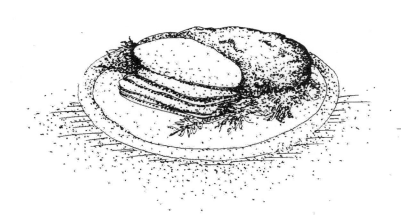

Beef Picante Skillet

1 pound lean ground beef
1 can tomato soup
1 cup chunky salsa or picante sauce
6 (6 inch) flour tortillas, cut into 1 inch pieces
1 ¼ cups shredded cheddar cheese

1. Cook beef in skillet until browned. Pour off fat.
2. Add soup, salsa, ¾ cup water, tortillas, ½ teaspoon salt and half the cheese. Heat to a boil. Cover and cook over low heat 5 minutes.
3. Top with remaining cheese. Serve right from the skillet.

Great Served With:
Sunny Yellow Squash • Marinated Black-Eyed Peas

Spiced Beef

1 pound lean ground beef
1 (1.25 ounce) package taco seasoning mix
1 (16 ounce) can Mexican stewed tomatoes, undrained
1 (16 ounce) can kidney beans, undrained
1 (1 pound) bag egg noodles

1. Cook beef in skillet; drain. Add taco seasoning and ½ cup water. Simmer 15 minutes.
2. Add the stewed tomatoes and kidney beans. You might want to add ¼ teaspoon salt.
3. Cook egg noodles following package directions. Serve spiced beef over noodles.

Great Served With: Pineapple Slaw

Asian Beef and Noodles

1 ¼ pound ground beef
2 (3 ounce) packages Oriental flavor instant
Ramen noodles
1 (16 ounce) package frozen Oriental Stir-Fry
mixture
½ teaspoon ground ginger
3 tablespoons thinly sliced green onions

1. In large skillet, brown ground beef. Drain. Add ½ cup water, salt and pepper and simmer 10 minutes. Transfer to a separate bowl.
2. In same skillet, combine 2 cups water, vegetables, noodles (broken up), ginger and both seasoning packets. Bring to a boil, reduce heat. Cover, simmer 3 minutes or until noodles are tender, stirring occasionally.
3. Return beef to skillet, stir in green onion. You can serve right from the skillet.

Great Served With: Spinach and Apple Salad

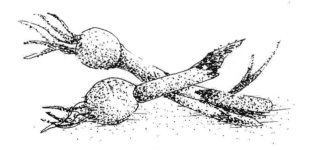

Pinto Bean Pie

1 pound lean ground beef
1 onion, chopped
2 (16 ounce) cans pinto beans, undrained
1 (10 ounce) can tomatoes and green chilies,
  undiluted
1 can French fried onion rings

1. In skillet, brown together the beef and onion; drain.
2. In a 2 quart casserole dish, layer 1 can beans, beef-onion mixture and one-half can of tomatoes and green chilies . Repeat layer.
3. Top with onion rings and bake, uncovered at 350 degrees for 30 minutes.

Great Served With:
Chili Cheese Squash • Easy Guacamole Salad

Chili Casserole

1 (40 ounce) can chili with beans
1 (4 ounce) can chopped green chilies
1 (2 ¼ ounce) can sliced ripe olives, drained
1 (8 ounce) package shredded cheddar cheese
2 cups ranch-flavored tortilla chips, crushed

1. In a bowl, combine all ingredients.
2. Transfer to a greased 3 quart casserole dish.
3. Bake, uncovered at 350 degrees for 35 minutes or until bubbly.

Great Served With:
Red Hot Onions • Shoe Peg Corn

Chili Pie

2 cups small corn chips
1 chopped onion
1 (19 ounce) can chili (without beans)
1 ½ cups grated cheddar cheese

1. In a 7 x 11 inch baking dish, place the corn chips; top with onion, then the chili and cheese.
2. Bake at 350 degrees for about 15 minutes.

Great Served With:
Baked Beans • Calypso Coleslaw

Easy Chili

2 pounds lean ground chuck
1 onion, chopped
4 (16 ounce) cans chili-hot beans, undrained
1 (1 ¾ ounce) packages chili seasoning mix
1 (46 ounce) can tomato juice

1. Cook beef and onion in a Dutch oven, stirring until meat crumbles; drain.
2. Stir in remaining ingredients.
3. Bring mixture to a boil; reduce heat and simmer, stirring occasionally for 2 hours.

Great Served With:
Corn Bread (Prepared with a Mix) • Broccoli Noodle Salad

Corned Beef Supper

1 (4 to 5 pound) corned beef brisket
4 large potatoes, peeled and quartered
6 carrots, peeled and halved
4 onions
1 head cabbage

1. Place corned beef in roaster, cover with water. Bring to a boil. Turn heat down and simmer 3 hours, adding water if necessary.
2. Add potatoes, carrots and onions. Cut cabbage into eighths and lay over top of other vegetables.
3. Bring to a boil; turn heat down and cook another 30 to 40 minutes, until vegetables are done. When slightly cool, slice corned beef across the grain.

Great Served With:
Cornbread (Prepared with a Mix) • Fantastic Fruit Salad

Oven Brisket

1 (5 to 6) pound trimmed brisket
1 package onion soup mix
1 (12 ounce) can Coke (not diet)
1 (10 ounce) bottle Heinz 57 sauce

1. Place brisket, fat side up, in a roasting pan.
2. In a bowl, combine onion mix, Coke and Heinz 57 sauce. Pour over brisket. Cover and cook at 325 degrees for 4 to 5 hours or until tender. Remove brisket from pan and pour off drippings. Chill both, separately, overnight.
3. The next day, trim all the fat from meat, slice and reheat. Skim the fat off the drippings and reheat; serve sauce over the brisket.

Great Served With:
Loaded Baked Potatoes • Broccoli-Cauliflower Salad

Smoked Brisket

1 (5 to 6 pound) trimmed brisket
1 bottle liquid smoke
Garlic and celery salt
1 onion, chopped
Worcestershire sauce
1 (6 ounce) bottle barbecue sauce

1. Place brisket in roaster. Pour liquid smoke over brisket.
   Sprinkle with garlic and celery salt; cover with onion.
   Cover and refrigerate overnight.
2. Before cooking, pour off liquid smoke and douse with
   Worcestershire.
3. Cover with foil and bake at 300 degrees for 5 hours.
   Uncover and pour barbecue sauce over brisket and bake
   another hour.

Great Served With:
Baked Beans • Broccoli Waldorf Salad

Great Brisket

2 onions, sliced
Paprika
Seasoned salt
1 (5 to 6 pound) trimmed brisket
1 (12 ounce) Pepsi-Cola

1. Place the onions in bottom of a roaster. Sprinkle with paprika and seasoned salt. Lay the brisket on top of onions and sprinkle more seasoned salt.
2. Bake, uncovered, at 450 degrees for ½ hour. Pour Pepsi over the roast and reduce oven to 325 degrees. Cover with foil and bake until tender, about 4 hours or until tender.
3. Baste occasionally with Pepsi and juices from brisket.

Great Served With:
Twice Baked Potatoes • Green Pea Salad

Sweet and Savory Brisket

1 (3 to 4 pound) trimmed beef brisket, cut in half
⅓ cup grape or plum jelly
1 cup ketchup
1 envelope onion soup mix
¾ teaspoon black pepper

1. Place half of the brisket in a slow cooker. In a bowl, combine the jelly, ketchup, soup mix and pepper. Spread half over meat.
2. Top with the remaining brisket and ketchup mixture. Cover and cook on low for 8 to 10 hours or until meat is tender.
3. Slice brisket; serve with the cooking juices.

Great Served With:
Macaroni, Cheese and Tomatoes • Easy Guacamole Salad

Heavenly Smoked Brisket

½ cup packed dark brown sugar
2 tablespoons Cajun seasoning
1 tablespoon lemon pepper
1 tablespoon Worcestershire sauce
1 (5 to 6 pound) beef brisket, untrimmed

1. Combine sugar, Cajun seasoning, pepper and Worcestershire in a shallow dish; add brisket, turning to coat both sides. Cover, chill 8 hours.
2. Soak Hickory wood chunks in water for 1 hour. Prepare charcoal fire in smoker; let burn 20 minutes. Drain chunks and place on coals. Place water pan in smoker; add water to pan to depth of fill line.
3. Remove brisket from marinade; place on lower food rack. Pour remaining marinade over meat. Cover with smoker lid. Cook 5 hours or until a meat thermometer inserted in thickest portion registers 170 degrees.

Great Served With:
Broccoli Cheese Potato Topper • Nutty Green Salad

Lemon Herb Pot Roast

1 (3 to 3 ½ pound) boneless beef chuck roast
1 teaspoon garlic powder
2 teaspoons lemon pepper
1 teaspoon dried basil
1 tablespoon oil

1. Combine garlic, lemon pepper and basil; press evenly into surface of beef.
2. In Dutch oven, heat oil over medium high heat until hot. Brown roast.
3. Add 1 cup water. Bring to a boil; reduce heat to low. Cover tightly; simmer for 3 hours. Vegetables can be added to roast the last hour of cooking.

Great Served With:
Marinated Corn Salad • Frozen Cherry Salad

Potato Beef Casserole

4 medium potatoes, peeled and sliced
1 ¼ pounds lean ground beef, browned and drained
1 can cream of mushroom soup
1 can condensed vegetable beef soup
½ teaspoon salt, ½ teaspoon pepper

1. In a large bowl, combine all ingredients. Transfer to a greased 3 quart baking dish.
2. Bake, covered at 350 degrees for 1 ½ hours or until potatoes are tender.

Great Served With:
Marinated Cucumbers • Cheesy Green Beans

Prime Rib of Beef

⅓ cup each chopped onion and celery
1 teaspoon salt
½ teaspoon garlic powder
1 beef rib roast (6 to 8 pounds)
1 (14 ounce) can beef broth

1. Combine onion and celery; place in a greased roasting pan. Combine salt, garlic powder and a little black pepper; rub over the roast. Place fat side up over vegetables.
2. Bake, uncovered at 350 degrees for 2 ½ to 3 ½ hours or until meat reaches desired doneness. (medium-rare, 145 degrees; medium, 160 degrees; well-done, 170 degrees)
3. Let stand for about 15 minutes before carving. Skim fat from pan drippings; add beef broth, stirring to remove browned bits. Heat. Strain, discarding vegetables. Serve au jus with the roast.

Great Served With:
Chive Potato Souffle • City Slicker Salad

Savory Rib Roast

1 tablespoon dried thyme
1 teaspoon dried rosemary, crushed
1 teaspoon rubbed sage
1 teaspoon pepper
1 beef rib roast (about 6 pounds)

1. In small bowl, combine the first 4 ingredients; rub over roast.
2. Place roast, fat side up, on a rack in a large roasting pan.
3. Bake uncovered at 350 degrees for 2 to 2 ½ hours or until meat reaches desired doneness (for rare, 140 degrees; medium, 160 degrees; and well done,170 degrees). Remove roast to a warm serving platter; let stand 10 minutes before slicing.

Great Served With:
Creamed Spinach Bake • Winter Salad

Shepherd's Pie

1 pound lean ground beef
1 envelope taco seasoning mix
1 cup shredded cheddar cheese
1 (11 ounce) can whole kernel corn, drained
2 cups mashed potatoes (use instant)

1. In skillet, brown beef; cook 10 minutes. Drain. Add taco seasoning and ¾ cup water; cook another 5 minutes.
2. Spoon beef mixture into an 8 inch baking pan. Sprinkle cheese on top, then corn. Spread mashed potatoes over top.
3. Bake at 350 degrees for 25 minutes or until top is golden.

Great Served With:
Broccoli –Cauliflower Salad • Cinniman Apple Salad

Delicious Meat Loaf

1 ½ pounds lean ground beef
⅔ cup Italian-seasoned dry breadcrumbs
2 eggs, beaten
1 can golden mushroom soup
2 tablespoons margarine

1. Mix beef, breadcrumbs, ½ the mushroom soup and egg thoroughly. In baking pan, shape firmly into a 8 x 4 inch loaf.
2. Bake at 350 degrees for 45 minutes.
3. In small saucepan, mix 2 tablespoons margarine, remaining soup and ¼ cup water. Heat thoroughly. Serve with meat loaf.

Great Served With:
Mixed Vegetables and Cheese • Marinated Black-Eyed Peas

Spanish Meatloaf

1 ½ pounds lean ground beef
1 (16 ounce) can Spanish rice
1 egg, beaten
¾ cup Ritz cracker crumbs
Chunky Salsa

1. Combine beef, rice, egg and crumbs. Shape into a loaf in a greased pan.
2. Bake at 350 degrees for 1 hour.
3. Serve with salsa on top of meat loaf.

Great Served With:
Super Corn Casserole • Marinated Cucumbers

Reuben Dogs

1 (27 ounce) can sauerkraut, rinsed and drained
2 teaspoons caraway seeds
8 hot dogs, halved lengthwise
1 cup shredded Swiss cheese
Thousand Island salad dressing

1. Place sauerkraut in a greased 2 quart baking dish. Sprinkle with caraway seeds. Top with hot dogs.
2. Bake uncovered at 350 degrees for 20 minutes or until heated through.
3. Sprinkle with cheese. Bake 3 to 5 minutes longer or until cheese is melted. Serve with salad dressing.

Great Served With:
Baked Beans • Serendipity Salad

Pineapple Pork Chops

6 to 8 thick boneless pork chops
1 (6 ounce) can frozen pineapple juice concentrate,
  thawed
3 tablespoons brown sugar
⅓ cup wine or tarragon vinegar
⅓ cup honey

1. Place pork chops in a skillet in a little oil and brown (I like to buy the boneless pork chops). Remove to a shallow baking dish.
2. Combine pineapple juice, sugar, vinegar and honey. Pour over pork chops.
3. Cook, covered at 325 degrees for about 50 minutes. Serve over hot rice.

Great Served With:
Green and Red Salad • Cauliflower Medley

Orange Pork Chops

6 to 8 medium thick pork chops
Flour
⅓ stick margarine
2 cups orange juice

1. Dip pork chops in flour and brown in skillet with the margarine. Place chops in a 9 x 13 inch baking pan, pouring remaining margarine over top of pork chops.
2. Pour orange juice over chops.
3. Cover and bake at 325 degrees for 55 minutes. Uncover for the last 15 minutes. Good served over hot rice.

Great Served With:
Pine Nut Green Beans • Sunflower Salad

Oven Pork Chops

6 to 8 medium thick pork chops
1 can cream of chicken soup
3 tablespoons catsup
1 tablespoon Worcestershire
1 medium onion, chopped

1. Brown pork chops in a little oil and season with salt and pepper. Place drained pork chops in a shallow baking dish.
2. In a saucepan, combine soup, catsup, Worcestershire and onion. Heat just enough to mix together. Pour over pork chops.
3. Bake, covered at 350 degrees for 50 minutes. Uncover the last 15 minutes.

Great Served With:
Sunny Yellow Squash • Broccoli Holiday Salad

Onion Smothered Pork Chops

1 tablespoon oil
6 pork chops, ½ inch thick
1 onion, chopped
2 tablespoons margarine
1 can cream of onion soup

1. In skillet, brown pork chops in oil and simmer about 10 minutes. Place pork chop in a greased shallow baking pan.
2. In the same skillet, add the margarine and sauté the chopped onion. The pan juices will be brown from the pork chops so your onions will also be browned from those juices already in skillet. Add the onion soup and ¼ cup water. Stirring well, your sauce will have a pretty light brown color.
3. Pour onion-soup mixture over pork chops. Cover and bake at 325 degrees for 40 minutes. Serve with Uncle Ben's brown rice.

Great Served With: Parmesan Broccoli • Sunflower Salad

Mexicali Pork Chops

1 envelope taco seasoning
4 boneless pork loin chops (½ inch thick)
1 tablespoon oil
Salsa

1. Rub taco seasoning over pork chops. In a skillet, brown pork chops in oil over medium heat.
2. Add 2 tablespoons water; turn heat to low and simmer pork chops about 40 minutes. Check to see if a little more water is needed.
3. Spoon salsa over pork chops to serve.

Great Served With:
Easy Guacamole Salad • Shoe Peg Corn

Pork Chops and Apples

6 thick cut pork chops
Four
Oil
3 baking apples

1. Dip pork chops in flour and coat well. In a skillet, brown pork chops in oil. Place in a 9 x 13 inch greased casserole.
2. Add about ⅓ cup water to casserole. Cook, covered at 325 degrees for about 50 minutes.
3. Peel, half and seed apples. Place ½ apple on top of each pork chop. Return to oven for about 10 minutes. (Don't overcook apples.)

Simple, easy and delicious!

Great Served With:
Carnival Couscous • Creamy Cranberry Salad

Pork Chops in Cream Gravy

4 pork chops, ¼ inch thick
Flour
Oil
2 ¼ cups whole milk

1. Trim all fat off pork chops. Dip chops in flour with a little salt and pepper. Brown pork chops on both sides in a little oil. Remove chops from skillet.
2. Add about 2 tablespoons flour to skillet and brown lightly; stir in a little salt and pepper. Slowly stir in milk to make gravy.
3 Return chops to skillet with the gravy. Cover and simmer on low burner for about 40 minutes. Serve over rice or noodles.

Grilled Pork Loin

1 (4 pound) boneless pork loin roast
1 (8 ounce) bottle Italian salad dressing
1 cup dry white wine
3 cloves garlic, minced
10 black peppercorns

1. Pierce roast at 1 inch intervals with fork; set aside. (Piercing allows marinade to penetrate the meat better.)
2. Combine salad dressing and remaining ingredients in a large plastic bag. Reserve ½ cup mixture for basing during grilling. Add roast to remaining mixture in bag. chill 8 hours, turning occasionally.
3. Remove roast from marinade, discarding marinade. Place roast on rack in cooking grill. Cook, covered with grill lid for 35 minutes or until meat thermometer inserted into thickest portion reaches 160 degrees; turning and basting with reserve ½ cup dressing mixture.

Great Served With: Herbed New Potatoes
Green Pea Salad

Apricot Baked Ham

1 (12 to 20 pound) whole ham, fully cooked
Whole cloves
2 tablespoons dry mustard
1 ¼ cups apricot jam
1 ¼ cups packed light brown sugar

1. Heat oven to 450 degrees. Place ham on a rack in a large roasting pan. Insert cloves in ham every inch or so.
2. Combine the dry mustard and the jam. Spread over entire surface of the ham. Pat the brown sugar over the jam mixture.
3. Reduce heat to 325 degrees. Bake uncovered at 15 minutes per pound.

This is the ham you will want for Easter dinner!

Great Served With: Mixed Vegetables and Cheese
Frozen Cranberry-Pineapple Salad

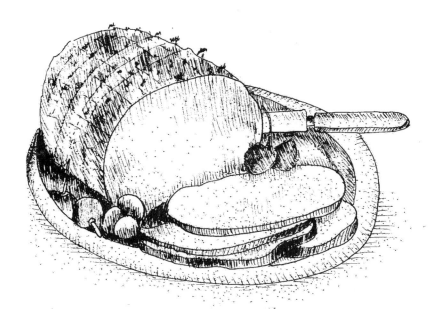

Baked Ham and Pineapple

1 fully cooked bone-in ham (6 to 8 pounds)
Whole cloves
½ cup packed brown sugar
1 (8 ounce) can sliced pineapple
5 maraschino cherries

1. Place ham in a roasting pan. Score the surface with shallow diagonal cuts, making diamond shapes; insert cloves into diamonds. Cover and bake at 325 degrees for 1 ½ hours.
2. Combine brown sugar and juice from the can of pineapple and pour over ham. Arrange pineapple slices and cherries on ham.
3. Bake, uncovered 40 minutes longer.

Great Served With:
Green Rice and Spinach • Cherry Cranberry Salad

Praline Ham

2 (½ inch thick) ham slices, cooked (about 2 ½ pounds)
½ cup maple syrup
3 tablespoons brown sugar
1 tablespoon margarine
⅓ cup chopped pecans

1. Bake ham slices in a shallow pan at 325 degrees for 10 minutes.
2. Bring syrup, sugar and margarine to a boil in a small saucepan, stirring often. Stir in pecans and spoon over ham.
3. Bake another 20 minutes.

Great Served With:
Carnival Couscous • Marinated Corn Salad

Grilled Ham and Apples

½ cup orange marmalade
2 teaspoons margarine
¼ teaspoon ground ginger
2 (½ inch thick) ham slices (about 2 ½ pounds)
4 apples, cut into ½ inch thick slices

1. Combine first 3 ingredients in a 1 cup glass measuring cup; microwave at HIGH 1 minute or until melted, stirring once.
2. Cook ham covered with the apples; cover the grill lid, over medium hot coals, turning occasionally and basting with marmalade mixture, about 20 minutes.

Great Served With:
Loaded Baked Potatoes • Broccoli-Cauliflower Salad

Peachy Glazed Ham

1 (16 ounce) can sliced peaches in light syrup, undrained
2 tablespoons dark brown sugar
2 teaspoon Dijon mustard
1 (1 pound) center-cut ham slice
⅓ cup sliced green onions

1. Drain peaches and reserve ½ cup syrup in a large skillet; set peaches aside.
2. Add sugar and mustard to skillet; bring to a boil over medium high heat. Cook 2 minutes or until slightly reduced.
3. Add ham and cook 2 minutes on each side. Add peaches and green onions; cover and cook over low heat 3 minutes or until peaches are thoroughly heated.

Great Served With:
Cauliflower Medley • Broccoli Noodle Salad

Ham with Orange Sauce

½ inch thick slice of fully cooked ham
1 cup orange juice
2 tablespoons brown sugar
1 ½ tablespoons cornstarch
⅓ cup white raisins

1. Place ham slice in shallow baking dish.
2. In a saucepan, combine orange juice, brown sugar, cornstarch and raisins. Bring to a boil, stirring constantly until mixture is slightly thick. Pour over ham slice.
3. Warm in 350 degree oven for about 20 minutes.

Great Served With:
Creamy Vegetable Casserole • Divinity Salad

Pineapple Sauce for Ham

Presliced and cooked honey baked ham slices
1 (15 ounce) can pineapple chunks, undrained
1 cup apricot preserves
1 ¼ cups packed brown sugar
¼ teaspoon cinnamon

1. Place ham slices in shallow baking pan. In a saucepan, combine pineapple preserves, brown sugar and cinnamon; heat.
2. Pour sauce over ham slices
3. Heat.

Great Served With:
Mediterranean Potato Salad • Asparagus Bake

Orange Sauce for Ham

⅔ **cup orange juice**
⅓ **cup water**
2 tablespoon brown sugar
1 ½ tablespoons cornstarch
⅓ **cup light raisins**

1. Mix all ingredients together in saucepan.
2. Heat and cook, stirring constantly until sauce thickens and is clear and bubbly.
3. Serve with precooked ham.

Dijon Baby Back Ribs

4 pounds baby back pork ribs
1 (12 ounce) bottle Dijon and Honey marinade
with lemon juice, divided

1. If needed, cut ribs in lengths to fit in large resealable plastic bag. Place ribs in bag and add ¾ cup marinade; seal bag and shake to coat. Marinate in refrigerator overnight.
2. Discard used marinade and place ribs on broiler pan sprayed with Pam.
3. Bake uncovered at 300 degrees for about 2 hours. Finish browning and cooking on grill, basting often with remaining marinade.

Tangy Apricot Ribs

3 to 4 pounds baby back pork loin ribs
1 (16 ounce) jar apricot preserves
⅓ cup soy sauce
¼ cup packed light brown sugar
2 teaspoons garlic powder

1. Place ribs in large roasting pan. Whisk preserves and next 3 ingredients until blended; pour over ribs. Cover and chill overnight.
2. Remove ribs from marinade, reserving marinade in a small saucepan. Line baking pan with foil; add ribs and sprinkle a little salt and pepper.
3. Bring marinade to a boil; cover, reduce heat and simmer 5 minutes. Bake ribs at 325 degrees for 1 hour and 30 minutes or until tender, basing frequently with marinade.

Great Served With:
Scalloped Potatoes • Broccoli Waldorf Salad.

Sweet and Sour Spareribs

3 to 4 pounds spareribs
3 tablespoons soy sauce
⅓ cup prepared mustard
1 cup packed brown sugar
½ teaspoon garlic salt

1. Place spareribs in roaster. Bake at 325 degrees for 45 minutes. Drain.
2. Make sauce with remaining ingredients and brush on ribs.
3. Return to oven, reduce heat to 300 degrees and bake for another hour or until tender. Baste several times while cooking.

Great Served With:
Creamy Mashed Potatoes • Broccoli Noodle Salad

Spunky Spareribs

5 to 6 pounds spareribs
1 (6 ounce) can frozen orange juice, undiluted
2 teaspoons Worcestershire sauce
½ teaspoon garlic powder

1. Place spareribs in a shallow baking pan, meaty side down. Sprinkle with a little salt and pepper. Roast at 375 degrees for 30 minutes. Turn ribs and roast another 15 minutes. Drain off fat.
2. Combine remaining ingredients and brush the mixture on ribs.
3. Reduce heat to 300 degrees. Cover ribs and roast 2 hours or until tender, basting occasionally.

Great Served With:
Twice Baked Potatoes • Winter Salad

Italian Sausage and Ravioli

1 pound sweet Italian pork sausage, casing
removed
1 (1 pound 10 ounce jar) extra chunky mushroom
and green pepper spaghetti sauce
1 (24 ounce) package frozen cheese-filled ravioli,
cooked and drained
Grated parmesan cheese

1. In a very large skillet over medium heat, cook sausage until browned and no longer pink. Stir to separate sausage or slice the sausage. Drain.
2. Stir in spaghetti sauce. Heat to boiling. Cook ravioli as package directs and add to spaghetti and sausage.
3. Sprinkle with parmesan cheese. Pour into serving dish.

Great Served With: Nutty Green Salad

Baked Applesauce

5 pounds tart green apples, peeled, cored, sliced
1 (8 ounce) jar plum jelly
½ cup sugar
⅓ cup lemon juice
¼ teaspoon ground nutmeg

1. Place apples in a 2 quart casserole. In saucepan, combine jelly, sugar and ⅔ cup water. Heat until jelly is melted. Remove from heat and stir in lemon juice and nutmeg. Pour over apples.
2. Bake, covered at 350 degrees for 1 hour and 15 minutes or until apples are soft. Delicious served with pork..

Cranberries and Apples

2 (21 ounce) cans pie apples
1 (16 ounce) can whole cranberry sauce
2 cups sugar
1 teaspoon ground cinnamon
Red food coloring, optional

1. In a large saucepan, mix together the apples, cranberry sauce, sugar and cinnamon. Add a few drops of red coloring.
2. Simmer for about 45 minutes, stirring occasionally.
3. Refrigerate to chill. Great served with pork.

Orange Roughy with Peppers

1 pound orange roughy
1 onion, sliced
2 red bell peppers, cut into julienne strips
1 teaspoon dried thyme leaves
¼ teaspoon black pepper

1. Cut fish into 4 serving pieces. Heat a little oil in a skillet. Layer onion and bell peppers in skillet. Sprinkle with half the thyme and pepper.
2. Place fish over peppers and sprinkle with remaining thyme and pepper.
3. Turn burner on high until fish is hot enough to begin cooking. Lower heat, cover and cook fish for 15 to 20 minutes or until fish flakes easily.

Great Served With:
Creamy Vegetable Casserole • Sunflower Salad

Lemon Dill Fish

½ cup mayonnaise
2 tablespoons lemon juice
½ teaspoon lemon peel
1 teaspoon dill weed
1 pound cod or flounder fillets

1. Combine mayonnaise, lemon juice, peel and dill until well blended.
2. Place fish on greased grill or broiler rack. Brush with half of sauce. Grill or broil 5 to 8 minutes; turn and brush with remaining sauce.
3. Continue grilling or broiling 5 to 8 minutes or until fish flakes easily with fork.

Great Served With:
Asparagus Bake • Broccoli Noodle Salad

Flounder Au Gratin

½ cup fine dry breadcrumbs
¼ cup grated parmesan cheese
1 pound flounder
⅓ cup mayonnaise

1. In shallow dish combine crumbs and cheese. Brush both sides of fish with the mayonnaise. Coat with crumb mixture.
2. Arrange in single layer in a shallow pan.
3. Bake at 375 degrees for 20 to 25 minutes or until fish flakes easily.

Great Served With:
Broccoli Stuffed Tomatoes • Scalloped Potatoes

Baked Fish

1 pound fish filets
Sauce: 3 tablespoons margarine
1 teaspoon tarragon
2 teaspoons capers
2 tablespoons lemon juice

1. Place fish filets in a greased shallow pan. Sprinkle with salt, pepper and a little margarine. Bake at 375 degrees for about 8 to 10 minutes; turn and bake another 6 minutes or until fish is flaky.
2. For sauce, melt margarine with the tarragon, caper and lemon juice. Serve over the warm fish.

Great Served With:
Carnival Couscous • Creamy Orange Salad

Spicy Catfish Amandine

½ stick margarine, melted
3 tablespoons lemon juice
6 to 8 catfish fillets
1 ½ teaspoons Creole seasoning
½ cup sliced almonds

1. Combine margarine and lemon juice; dip each fillet in margarine mixture. Arrange in a 9 x 13 inch baking dish.
2. Sprinkle fish with Creole seasoning.
3. Bake at 375 degrees for 25 to 30 minutes or until fish flakes easily when tested with a fork. Sprinkle almonds over fish for the last 5 minutes of baking.

Great Served With:
Macaroni, Cheese and Tomatoes • Pineapple Slaw

Golden Catfish Fillets

3 eggs
¾ cup flour
¾ cup cornmeal
1 teaspoon garlic powder
6 to 8 catfish fillets (4 to 8 ounces each)

1. In a shallow bowl, beat eggs until foamy. In another shallow bowl, combine flour cornmeal, seasonings and a little salt.
2. Dip fillets in eggs, then coat with cornmeal mixture.
3. Heat ¼ inch oil in a large skillet; fry fish over medium-high heat for about 4 minutes on each side or until fish flakes easily with a fork.

Great Served With:
Baked Beans • Broccoli-Cauliflower Salad

Curried Red Snapper

1 ½ pounds fresh red snapper
2 medium onions, chopped
2 celery ribs, chopped
1 teaspoon curry powder
¼ cup milk

1. Place snapper in a greased 9 x 13 inch baking pan.
2. In skillet, saute onions and celery in a little margarine. Add curry powder, a little salt; mixing well. Remove from heat; stir in milk. Spoon over snapper.
3. Bake, uncovered at 350 degrees for 25 minutes or until fish flakes easily with a fork.

Great Served With:
Mixed Vegetables and Cheese • Serendipity Salad

Chipper Fish

2 pounds sole or orange roughy
½ cup Caesar salad dressing
1 cup crushed potato chips
½ cup shredded cheddar cheese

1. Dip fish in dressing. Place in a greased baking dish.
2. Combine chips and cheese; sprinkle over fish.
3. Bake at 375 degrees for about 20 to 25 minutes.

Great Served With:
Almond Green Beans • Marinated Cucumbers

Shrimp Newburg

1 can condensed cream of shrimp soup
¼ cup water
1 teaspoon seafood seasoning
1 (1 pound) package frozen cooked salad shrimp,
**   thawed**

1. In a saucepan, combine soup, water and seafood season-ing. Bring to a boil; reduce heat and stir in shrimp. Heat thoroughly.
2. Serve over hot white rice.

Great Served With:
Spinach and Apple Salad • Best Cauliflower

Shrimp Scampi

2 pounds raw shrimp, peeled
1 stick butter (must be butter)
3 cloves garlic, pressed
¼ cup lemon juice
Tabasco sauce

1. Melt butter and saute garlic; add lemon juice and a few dashes of Tabasco.
2. Arrange shrimp in a single layer in a shallow pan. Pour garlic butter over shrimp and salt lightly.
3. Broil 2 minutes; turn shrimp and broil 2 more minutes. Reserve garlic butter and serve separately.

Great Served With:
Pine Nut Green Beans • City Slicker Salad

Skillet Shrimp Scampi

2 teaspoons olive oil
2 pounds uncooked shrimp, peeled and deveined
⅔ cup Lawry's herb and garlic marinade with lemon juice
¼ cup finely chopped green onion, tops too

1. In large nonstick skillet, heat oil. Add shrimp and marinade.
2. Cook, stirring often until shrimp turns pink. Stir in green onions.
3. Serve over hot, cooked rice or your favorite pasta.

Great Served With:
Cheesy Green Beans • Broccoli-Cauliflower Salad

Your Guide to Left-Over Turkey, Chicken and Ham

Add 3 cups cubed chicken or turkey to Salads I-VIII

Chicken or Turkey Salad I

⅔ **cup chopped celery**
¾ **cup sweet pickle relish**
1 bunch fresh green onions, chopped, tops too
3 hard-boiled eggs, chopped
¾ **cup mayonnaise**

1. Combine the 3 cups of chopped chicken, celery, relish, onions and eggs.
2. Toss with the mayonnaise.
3. Refrigerate. Serve on a lettuce leaf.

Chicken or Turkey Salad II

⅔ **cup chopped celery**
⅔ **cup toasted slivered almonds**
2 small, firm bananas, sliced
1 (8 ounce) can pineapple tidbits, drained
¾ **cup mayonnaise**

1. Combine the 3 cups of chopped chicken, celery, almonds, bananas and pineapple.
2. Toss with mayonnaise.
3. Refrigerate. Serve on a lettuce leaf.

Add 3 cups cubed chicken or turkey to Salads I-VIII

Chicken or Turkey Salad III

1 cup chopped celery
1 cup tart green apple, peeled and cubed
1 (10 ounce) can mandarin oranges, drained
¾ cup chopped macadamia nuts
1 teaspoon curry powder, ¾ cup mayonnaise

1. Combine the 3 cups chopped chicken, celery, apple, oranges and nuts.
2. Toss with the curry powder and mayonnaise.
3. Refrigerate. Serve on a lettuce leaf.

Chicken or Turkey Salad IV

1 cup celery
1 ½ cup green grapes, cut in half
¾ cup cashew nuts
¾ cup mayonnaise
1 cup chow mein noodles

1. Combine the 3 cups chopped chicken, celery, grapes and cashew nuts.
2. Toss with the mayonnaise. Just before serving, mix in the noodles.
3. Serve on a cabbage leaf.

Add 3 cups cubed chicken or turkey to Salads I-VIII

Chicken or Turkey Salad V

⅔ cup chopped celery, ½ cup chopped pecans
⅔ cup chopped sweet yellow bell pepper
1 bunch fresh green onions, chopped, tops too
⅔ cup pickle relish
⅔ cup mayonnaise

1. Combine the 3 cups chopped chicken, celery, pecans, bell pepper, onions and relish.
2. Toss with mayonnaise
3. Refrigerate.
   Serve on shredded lettuce.

Chicken or Turkey Salad VI

⅔ cup celery
1 can sliced water chestnuts
1 ½ cup seedless red grapes, cut in halves
⅔ cup chopped pecans
¾ cup mayonnaise, ½ teaspoon curry powder

1. Combine the 3 cups chopped chicken, celery, water chestnuts, grapes and pecans.
2. Toss with the mayonnaise and curry powder.
3. Serve on a cabbage leaf.

Add 3 cups cubed chicken or turkey to Salads I-VIII

Chicken or Turkey Salad VII

1 (6 ounce) box long grain and wild rice, cooked,
   drained
1 bunch fresh green onions, chopped, tops too
1 cup chopped walnuts
1 (8 ounce) can sliced water chestnuts
1 cup mayonnaise, ¾ cup curry powder

1. Combine the 3 cups chopped chicken, rice, onions, walnuts
   and water chestnuts.
2. Toss with the mayonnaise and curry powder.
3. Refrigerate. Serve on a a bed of lettuce.

Chicken or Turkey Salad VIII

⅔ cup chopped celery
1 (15 ounce) can pineapple tidbits
¾ cup slivered almonds
¾ cup chopped red bell pepper
⅔ cup mayonnaise

1. Combine the 3 cups chopped chicken, celery, pineapple,
   almonds and bell pepper.
2. Toss with mayonnaise.
3. Refrigerate. Serve on a lettuce leaf.

Add 3 cups chopped chicken or turkey to Casseroles I-VI

Chicken Casserole I

1 (16 ounce) package frozen broccoli flowerets, thawed
1 can cream of chicken soup, diluted with ¼ cup water
⅔ cup mayonnaise
1 cup shredded cheddar cheese
1 ½ cups crushed cheese crackers

1. Combine chicken, broccoli, soup, mayonnaise and cheese. Mix well
2. Pour into a buttered 3 quart casserole. Spread cheese crackers over top.
3. Bake uncovered at 350 degrees for 40 minutes.

Chicken Casserole II

1 (4 ounce) can sliced mushrooms, drained
1 can cream of chicken soup, diluted with ¼ cup water
1 (8 ounce) carton sour cream
⅓ cup cooking sherry
1 envelope dry onion soup mix

1. Combine chicken, mushrooms, soup, sour cream, sherry and onion soup mix.
2. Pour into a buttered 3 quart casserole.
3. Bake covered at 350 degrees for 40 minutes. Serve over hot white rice.

Add 3 cups chopped chicken or turkey to Casseroles I-VI

Chicken Casserole III

**1 (6.9 ounce) box chicken Rice-A-Roni, cooked
  according to directions
1 can cream of mushroom soup
1 can cream of celery soup
1 (10 ounce) package frozen green peas, thawed
1 cup shredded cheddar cheese**

1. Combine cooked Rice-A-Roni, soups, peas, cheese and ½ cup water. Mix well.
2. Pour into a buttered 3 quart casserole.
3. Bake covered at 350 degrees for 40 minutes.

Chicken Casserole IV

**1 (10 ounce) bag Doritos
1 onion, chopped
1 can cream of chicken soup
2 (10 ounce) cans tomatoes and green chilies
1 pound box Velveeta cheese, cut in chunks**

1. Place ½ the Doritos in a Pam sprayed 9 x 13 inch baking dish. Crush a little with the palm of your hand. In a large saucepan, combine onion, soup, tomatoes and cheese. Heat on medium, stirring, until cheese is melted. Add the 3 cups of chicken; pour over Doritos.
2. Crush remaining Doritos in a baggie with a rolling pin. Sprinkle over chicken-cheese mixture.
3. Bake uncovered at 350 degrees about 40 minutes or until bubbly around edges.

Add 3 cups chopped chicken or turkey to Casseroles I-VI

Chicken Casserole V

2 cans cream of mushroom soup
1 soup can milk, 2 teaspoons curry powder
1 (4 ounce) can sliced mushrooms, drained
2 ½ cups cooked rice (use instant)
3 cooked, crisp bacon slices, chopped

1. In a large saucepan, combine the 3 cups chicken and all remaining ingredients.
2. Pour into a 9 x 13 inch Pam sprayed baking dish.
3. Bake covered at 350 degrees for 40 minutes.

Chicken Casserole VI

1 can cream of celery soup
1 (8 ounce) carton sour cream
1 package onion soup mix (dry)
1 (8 ounce) can green peas, drained
2 cups cracker crumbs

1. In a large saucepan, combine the 3 cups chicken, soup, sour cream and onion soup mix. Heat just enough to mix well.
2. Add the green peas and spoon into a buttered 3 quart baking dish. Sprinkle crumbs over top of casserole.
3. Bake uncovered at 350 degrees for 35 minutes or until bubbly.

Add 3 cups chopped ham to Salads I-V

Ham Salad I

½ cup chopped celery
1 bunch fresh green onions, chopped, tops too
⅓ cup sweet pickle relish
1 teaspoon mustard, ⅔ cup mayonnaise
1 (15 ounce) can shoestring potato sticks

1. Combine chopped ham, celery, onions and relish.
2. Toss with the mustard and mayonnaise.
3. Refrigerate. When ready to serve, fold in potato sticks. Serve on a cabbage leaf.

Ham Salad II

1 bunch fresh green onions, chopped, tops too
½ cup toasted silvered almonds
½ cup sunflower seeds
2 cups chopped fresh broccoli flowerets
¾ cup mayonnaise

1. Combine chopped ham, green onions, almonds, sunflower seeds and broccoli flowerets.
2. Toss with mayonnaise.
3. Refrigerate. Serve on lettuce leaves.

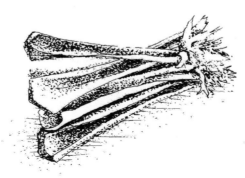

Add 3 cups chopped ham to Salads I-V

Ham Salad III

1 (15 ounce) can pinto beans, drained
½ large purple onion, chopped
1 (11 ounce) can Mexicorn, drained
1 cup chopped celery
About ½ to ¾ of an 8 ounce bottle Italian dressing

1. Combine chopped ham, beans, onion, corn and celery.
2. Toss with salad dressing.
3. Refrigerate. Serve on a bed of shredded lettuce.

Ham Salad IV

¾ cup chopped celery
1 cup small curd cottage cheese, drained
1 cup cut-up cauliflower flowerets
1 cup cut-up broccoli flowerets
Prepared Honey Mustard dressing

1. Combine chopped ham, celery, cottage cheese, cauliflower and broccoli.
2. Toss with dressing.
3. Refrigerate. Serve on lettuce leaves.

Ham Salad V

⅔ cup chopped celery
1 (15 ounce) can English peas
1 red bell pepper, chopped
8 ounces mozzarella cheese, cut in chunks
¾ cup garlic mayonnaise

1. Combine the ham, celery, peas, bell pepper and cheese.
2. Toss with garlic mayonnaise.
3. Refrigerate. Serve on cabbage leaves.

**And a few more recipes to use with left-over
Turkey, Chicken or Ham**

Chicken (or Turkey) Jambalaya

1 (15 ounce) can stewed tomatoes, undrained
1 package Knorr vegetable soup and dip dry mix
¾ teaspoon crushed red pepper
2 cups chopped chicken or turkey
1 cup ham, cut into matchsticks

1. In a large skillet, combine tomatoes, 2 cups water, soup mix and red pepper. Bring to a boil, stirring well.
2. Reduce heat, cover and simmer 15 minutes.
3. Stir in chicken or turkey; cook 5 minutes longer. Serve over hot white, cooked rice.

Turkey and Dressing Pie (or Chicken)

1 (6 ounce) box Stove Top stuffing mix
3 tablespoons margarine, melted
2 ½ cups finely chopped cooked turkey or chicken
1 cup shredded cheddar cheese
4 eggs, beaten
2 cups half and half

1. Combine dressing, seasoning packet and margarine; mix well. Press on bottom and sides of a buttered 2 quart baking dish. Bake at 400 degrees for 5 minutes. Cool
2. Combine turkey and cheese; spread over dressing mixture in pan. Combine eggs and half and half; beat well. Pour over turkey mixture.
3. Reduce oven to 325 degrees. Bake uncovered for 35 to 40 minutes or until set.

Golden Chicken (or Turkey) Casserole

2 ½ cups cubed cooked chicken or turkey
1 (8 ounce) can pineapple chunks or tidbits,
drained
½ cup apricot preserves
1 can cream of chicken soup, undiluted
1 (8 ounce) can sliced water chestnuts

1. In a bowl, combine all ingredients, plus ⅓ cup water, mixing well. Transfer to a buttered 2 quart baking dish.
2. Bake uncovered at 350 degrees for 35 minutes or until thoroughly heated.
3. Serve over hot cooked rice.

Ranch Pasta and Turkey (or Chicken)

1 (8 ounce) package your favorite pasta
1 stick margarine
1 packet Hidden Valley Ranch dressing dry mix
1 (16 ounce) can peas and carrots, undrained
3 cups cubed turkey or chicken

1. Cook pasta as directed on package. In a saucepan, combine margarine, dressing mix, peas and carrots. Heat until margarine has melted.
2. Toss with pasta and turkey. Place in a 2 quart casserole.
3. Heat at 350 degrees for about 20 minutes. (If you like, you can sprinkle some grated cheese over top – after the casserole has baked.)

Chicken (or Turkey) Broccoli Casserole

1 can cream of chicken soup
¾ cup of milk
3 cups diced cooked chicken
1 (10 ounce) box broccoli spears, thawed
1 (16 ounce) box chicken stuffing mix (prepare
   according to direction)

1. Heat soup and milk, just enough to be able to mix well. Pour into a greased 9 x 13 inch baking dish.
2. Layer chicken over the soup; place the broccoli on top. Top with stuffing mix.
3. Bake covered at 350 degrees for 50 minutes.

Ham and Potato Casserole

1 (24 ounce) package frozen hash browns with
   onion and peppers
3 cups bite-size chunks of cooked ham
1 can cream of chicken soup
1 can cream of celery soup
1 (8 ounce) package shredded cheddar cheese

1. In a large bowl, combine first four ingredients, plus ⅓ cup water, some salt and pepper. Spoon into a Pam sprayed 9 x 13 inch baking dish.
2. Bake covered at 350 degrees for 40 minutes.
3. Remove from oven, uncover and sprinkle cheese over casserole and bake another 5 minutes.

Ham (or Beef) Spread

2 cups ham or roast beef
¾ cup sweet pickle relish
2 celery ribs, finely chopped
2 hard-boiled eggs, chopped
½ onion, finely chopped, mayonnaise

1. Chop meat in food processor and add relish, celery, eggs and onion; adding a little salt and pepper.
2. Fold in enough mayonnaise to make mixture spreadable.
3. Refrigerate. Spread on crackers or bread for sandwiches.

Ham'N Cheese Mashed Potatoes

2 cups mashed potatoes (use instant)
¾ teaspoon garlic powder
2 cups diced, cooked ham
1 (8 ounce) package shredded cheddar cheese
½ cup whipping cream

1. In a bowl, combine the potatoes and garlic powder. Spread in a buttered 2 quart baking dish.
2. Sprinkle with the ham. Fold cheese into the whipping cream and spoon over ham.
3. Bake uncovered at 400 degrees for 15 minutes or until golden brown.

Ham and Broccoli Stromboli

1 (10 ounce) package refrigerated pizza dough
1 (10 ounce) package chopped broccoli
1 can cream of celery soup
3 cups diced, cooked ham
1 cup shredded cheddar cheese

1. Unroll dough onto greased baking sheet. Set aside. Cook broccoli according to package directions.
2. Mix together the broccoli, soup and ham. Spread ham mixture down center of dough. Top with cheese. Fold long sides of dough over filling; pinch and seal. Pinch short side to seal.
3. Bake uncovered at 400 degrees for 20 minutes or until golden brown. Slice and serve.

Hamwiches

1 (8 ounce) can refrigerated crescent rolls
2 tablespoons mayonnaise
2 teaspoons prepared mustard
1 ¼ cups finely chopped, cooked ham
½ cup shredded Swiss cheese

1. Unroll dough and separate into 4 rectangles; press seams to seal.
2. Combine mayonnaise and mustard; spread over rectangles, leaving a ½ inch border. Sprinkle ham and cheese evenly over half of each rectangle; moisten edges with water. Fold dough over and pinch edges to seal.
3. Bake at 375 degrees for 10 to 15 minutes or until puffed and golden.

SWEETS

Favorite Cake

1 box yellow cake mix
3 eggs
1 1⅓ cup oil
1 (9.9 ounce) box Betty Crocker coconut pecan icing mix (this is a dry mix)

1. In mixer bowl, combine cake mix, eggs, 1 ¼ cups water and oil. Beat well.
2. Stir in the box of icing mix. Pour into a greased and floured bundt pan.
3. Bake at 350 degrees for 45 minutes. Test with a toothpick.

Some grocery stores do not carry this coconut pecan icing but this cake is worth looking for the icing. You can keep all these ingredients right in your pantry – to have on hand when you need to take food to a friend.

Cherry-Pineapple Cake

1 (20 ounce) can crushed pineapple, drained
1 can cherry pie filling
1 (18 ounce) yellow cake mix
2 sticks margarine, softened
1 ¼ cups chopped pecans

1. Place all ingredients in mixing bowl. Mix by hand.
2. Pour into a greased and floured 9 x 13 inch baking dish.
3. Bake at 350 degrees for one hour and 10 minutes.

Easy Pineapple Cake

2 cups sugar
2 cups flour
1 (20 ounce) can crushed pineapple, undrained
1 teaspoon baking soda
1 teaspoon vanilla

1. Mix by hand; combine all cake ingredients. Pour into a greased and floured 9 x 13 inch baking pan.
2. Bake at 350 degrees for 30 to 35 minutes.

Don't worry–this is right–there are <u>no</u> eggs in this recipe!

Easy Pineapple Cake Icing

1 (8 ounce) package cream cheese, softened
1 stick margarine, melted
1 cup powdered sugar
1 cup chopped pecans

1. Beat with mixer the cream cheese, margarine and powdered sugar. Add the chopped pecans and pour over HOT cake.

Strawberry Pound Cake

1 box strawberry cake mix
1 (3 ½ ounce) package instant pineapple pudding
mix (or coconut cream)
⅓ cup oil
4 eggs
1 (3 ounce) package strawberry gelatin

1. Mix all ingredients plus 1 cup water and beat for 2 minutes at medium speed. Pour into a greased and floured bundt pan.
2. Bake at 325 degrees for 55 to 60 minutes. Cake is done when toothpick comes out clean.
3. Cool for 20 minutes before removing cake from pan. If you would like an icing, use a commercial vanilla icing.

Two – Surprise Cake

1 bakery orange chiffon cake
1 (15 ounce) can crushed pineapple, undrained
1 (3.4 ounce) package vanilla instant pudding
1 (8 ounce) carton Cool Whip
½ cup slivered almonds, toasted

1. Slice cake horizontally, making 3 layers.
2. Mix pineapple, pudding and Cool Whip together; blending well.
3. Spread on each layer and then cover top of cake. Sprinkle almonds on top. Refrigerate.

The 1st surprise is how easy it is and the 2nd surprise is how good it is! You'll make this more than once in this lifetime.

Chocolate Orange Cake

1 (16 ounce) loaf frozen pound cake, thawed
1 (12 ounce) jar orange marmalade
1 (16 ounce) can ready to spread chocolate-fudge
   frosting

1. Cut cake horizontally into 3 layers. Place one layer on cake platter. Spread with ½ of the marmalade. Place second layer over first and spread on remaining marmalade.
2. Top with third cake layer and spread frosting liberally on top and sides of cake.
3. Refrigerate.

Poppy Seed Bundt Cake

1 package yellow cake mix
1 (3.4 ounce) package instant coconut cream
   pudding mix
½ cup oil
3 eggs
2 tablespoons poppy seeds

1. In mixing bowl, combine cake and pudding mixes, 1 cup water, oil and eggs. Beat on low speed until moistened. Beat on medium speed for 2 minutes.
2. Stir in poppy seeds. Pour into a greased and floured bundt pan.
3. Bake at 350 degrees for 50 minutes or until a toothpick inserted near the center comes out clean. Cool for 10 minutes; remove from pan. Dust with powdered sugar.

Blueberry Pound Cake

1 box yellow cake mix
1 (8 ounce) package cream cheese, softened
½ cup oil
4 eggs
1 (15 ounce) can whole blueberries, drained

1. With mixer, combine all ingredients and beat for 3 minutes. Pour into a greased and floured bundt or tube pan.
2. Bake at 350 degrees for 50 minutes. Test with toothpick to be sure cake is done.
3. Sprinkle powdered sugar over top of cake.

Cherry Cake

1 box French vanilla cake mix, dry
1 stick margarine, melted
2 eggs
1 can cherry pie filling
1 cup chopped pecans

1. In a large bowl, mix by hand, all ingredients.
2. Pour into a greased and floured bundt or tube pan.
3. Bake at 350 degrees for one hour. You could sprinkle powdered sugar on top of cake.

Chocolate Cherry Cake

1 milk chocolate cake mix
1 can cherry pie filling
3 eggs

1. In mixing bowl, combine cake mix, pie filling and eggs. Mix by hand. Pour into a greased and floured 9 x 13 inch baking dish.
2. Bake at 350 degrees for 35 to 40 minutes. Test with toothpick for doneness.

Chocolate Cherry Cake Frosting

5 tablespoons margarine
1 ¼ cups sugar
½ cup milk
1 (6 ounce) package chocolate chips

3. When cake is done combine margarine, sugar and milk in a medium saucepan. Boil one minute, stirring constantly. Add chocolate chips and stir until chips are melted. Pour over hot cake.

This is a chocolate lover's dream.

Hawaiian Dream Cake

1 yellow cake mix
4 eggs
¾ cup oil
½ (20 ounce) can crushed pineapple, with ½ the juice

1. With mixer beat together all ingredients for 4 minutes.
2. Pour into a greased and floured 9 x 13 inch baking pan.
3. Bake at 350 degrees for 30 to 35 minutes or until cake tests done with toothpick. Cool.

Hawaiian Dream Cake Coconut Pineapple Icing

½ (20 ounce) can crushed pineapple with juice
1 stick margarine
1 (16 ounce) box powdered sugar
1 can coconut

1. Heat together the pineapple and margarine. Boil 2 minutes. Add powdered sugar and coconut. Punch holes in cake with knife. Pour hot icing over cake.

This looks like a lot of trouble to make, but it really isn't –
and it is a wonderful cake!

Old Fashioned Applesauce Spice Cake

1 box spice cake mix
3 eggs
1 ¼ cups applesauce
⅓ cup oil
1 cup chopped pecans

1. With mixer, combine cake mix, eggs, applesauce and oil. Beat at medium speed for 2 minutes. Stir in pecans.
2. Pour into a 9 x 13 inch greased and floured baking pan. Bake at 350 degrees for 40 minutes. Test until toothpick comes out clean. Cool.
3. For frosting, use a prepared vanilla frosting, adding ½ teaspoon cinnamon.

This cake would also be good with the Coconut Pineapple Icing on page ???.

Coconut Cake Deluxe

1 package yellow cake mix (plus ingredients called for in cake mix)
1 can sweetened condensed milk
1 can coconut cream
1 can coconut
1 (8 ounce) carton Cool Whip

1. Mix yellow cake according to directions. Pour into a greased and floured 9 x 13 inch baking pan. Bake in a 350 degree oven for 30 to 35 minutes or until toothpick inserted in center comes out clean.
2. While cake is warm, punch holes in cake about 2 inches apart. Pour sweetened condensed milk over cake and spread around until all milk has soaked into cake. Then pour the can of coconut cream over cake and sprinkle the coconut on top.
3. Let cool and frost with Cool Whip. Refrigerate.

This is a fabulous cake!

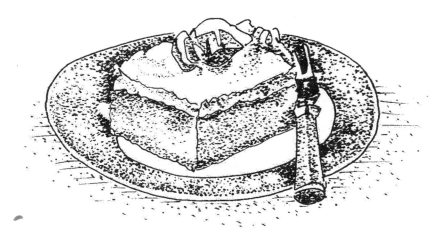

Gooey Butter Cake

1 box butter cake mix
1 stick margarine, melted
4 eggs, divided
1 (16 ounce) box powdered sugar (reserve ¾ cup for top)
1 (8 ounce) package cream cheese, softened

1. With mixer, beat together 2 eggs with cake mix and margarine. Spread mixture into a greased and floured 9 x 13 inch baking pan.
2. Mix together the sugar (except for the ¾ cup), 2 remaining eggs and cream cheese. Beat until smooth. Spread mixture on top of dough. Sprinkle remaining sugar on top.
3. Bake cake at 350 degrees for 40 minutes. Cake will puff up and then go down when cake is cooled.

Angel Cream Cake

1 large angel food cake
1 (18 ounce) jar chocolate ice cream topping
½ gallon vanilla ice cream, softened (or Cookies and Cream)
1 (12 ounce) carton Cool Whip
½ cup slivered almonds, toasted

1. Tear cake into large pieces. Stir in chocolate topping to coat pieces of cake. Mix in softened ice cream. Work fast! Stir into a tube pan and freeze overnight.
2. Turn out onto large cake plate and frost with Cool Whip. Decorate with almonds. Freeze.

Angel Strawberry Delight Cake

1 cup sweetened condensed milk
¼ cup lemon juice
1 pint fresh strawberries, cut in half
1 angel food cake
1 pint heavy cream, whipped

1. Combine condensed milk and lemon juice. Fold in strawberries.
2. Slice cake in half. Spread strawberry filling on bottom layer. Place top layer over filling.
3. Cover with whipped cream and top with extra strawberries.

Golden Rum Cake

1 box yellow cake mix with pudding
3 eggs
⅓ cup oil
½ cup rum
1 cup chopped pecans

1. Mix together in mixer the cake mix, eggs, water, oil and rum; blending well.
2. Stir in pecans. Pour into a greased and floured 10 inch tube or bundt pan.
3. Bake at 325 degrees for 1 hour. You might want to sprinkle powdered sugar over cooled cake.

Chess Cake

1 box yellow cake mix
2 eggs
1 stick margarine, softened
Topping: 2 eggs
1 (8 ounce) package cream cheese, softened
1 (1 pound) box powdered sugar

1. Beat together the cake mix, 2 eggs and margarine. Press into a greased 9 x 13 inch baking pan.
2. Beat together the 2 eggs, cream cheese and powdered sugar. Pour over cake.
3. Bake at 350 degrees for 35 minutes.

Pound Cake

2 sticks butter, softened (not margarine)
2 cups sugar
5 eggs
2 cups flour
1 tablespoon almond flavoring

1. Combine all ingredients in mixer and beat for 10 minutes at medium speed.
2. Pour into greased and floured tube pan (batter will be very thick).
3. Bake at 325 degrees for one hour. Test with toothpick for doneness.

Pound Cake Deluxe

1 bakery pound cake
1 (15 ounce) can crushed pineapple, undrained
1 (3.4 ounce) package coconut instant pudding
  mix
1 (8 ounce) carton Cool Whip
½ cup coconut

1. Slice cake horizontally making 3 layers.
2. Mix pineapple, pudding and Cool Whip together, blending well.
3. Spread on each layer and sprinkle top of cake with the coconut. Refrigerate.

Pineapple Angel Cake

1 (1-step) angel food cake mix
1 (20 ounce) can crushed pineapple, undrained

1. Place angel food cake mix in mixing bowl and pour pineapple in. Beat as directed on cake mix box.
2. Pour into an ungreased 9 x 13 inch baking pan.
3. Bake at 350 degrees for 30 minutes. This is a good low calorie cake, but if you want it iced, use a prepared vanilla icing.

Quick Fruitcake

**1 (15.6 ounce) package cranberry or blueberry
  quick bread mix**
½ cup chopped pecans
½ cup chopped dates
¼ cup chopped maraschino cherries
¼ cup crushed pineapple, drained

1. Prepare quick bread batter according to package directions. Stir in remaining ingredients. Pour into a 9 x 5 inch greased loaf pan.
2. Bake at 350 degrees for 60 minutes or until a toothpick inserted in cake comes out clean. Cool 10 minutes before removing from pan.

Easy Cheesecake

2 (8 ounce) packages cream cheese, softened
½ cup sugar
½ teaspoon vanilla
2 eggs
1 (9 inch) graham cracker pie crust

1. In mixer, beat together the cream cheese, sugar, vanilla and eggs.
2. Pour into pie crust.
3. Bake at 350 degrees for 40 minutes. Cool. Serve with any pie filling.

Cranberry Coffee Cake

2 eggs
1 cup mayonnaise
1 box spice cake mix
1 (16 ounce) can whole cranberry sauce
Powdered sugar

1. With mixer beat together eggs, mayonnaise and cake mix; mixing well. Fold in cranberry sauce.
2. Pour into a greased and floured 9 x 13 inch baking pan.
3. Bake at 325 degrees for 45 minutes. Test with toothpick to be sure cake is done. When cake is cool, dust with powdered sugar. If you would rather have an icing rather than the powdered sugar, use a prepared icing.

Sunny Lime Pie

2 (6 ounce) cartons key lime pie yogurt
1 (3 ounce) package lime gelatin, dry
1 (8 ounce) carton Cool whip
1 (9 inch) graham cracker pie crust

1. In a bowl, combine yogurt and lime gelatin; mixing well.
2. Fold in Cool Whip and spread in pie crust.
3. Freeze. Take out of freezer 20 minutes before slicing.

Nothing could be easier!

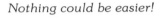

Creamy Lemon Pie

1 (8 ounce) package cream cheese, softened
1 can sweetened condensed milk
¼ cup lemon juice
1 can lemon pie filling
1 (9 inch) graham cracker pie crust

1. In mixing bowl, cream cheese until creamy. Add sweetened condensed milk and lemon juice. Beat until mixture is very creamy.
2. Fold in lemon pie filling, stirring well.
3. Pour into pie crust. Refrigerate several hours before slicing and serving.

Cherry Pecan Pie

1 can sweetened condensed milk
¼ cup lemon juice
1 (8 ounce) carton Cool Whip
1 cup chopped pecans
1 can cherry pie filling

1. Combine condensed milk and lemon juice; stirring well. Fold in Cool Whip.
2. Fold pecans and pie filling into mixture.
3. Spoon into 2 graham cracker crusts. Chill overnight.

Chocolate Cream Cheese Pie

1 (8 ounce) package cream cheese, softened
¾ cup powdered sugar
¼ cup cocoa
1 (8 ounce) container Cool Whip, thawed
½ cup chopped pecans

1. Combine first 3 ingredients in a mixing bowl; beat at medium speed until creamy.
2. Add Cool Whip, folding until smooth.
3. Spread in a prepared crumb pie crust and sprinkle pecans over top. Refrigerate.

Coffee Mallow Pie

1 tablespoon instant coffee granules
4 cups miniature marshmallows
1 tablespoon margarine
1 (8 ounce) carton whipping cream, whipped
½ cup chopped walnuts, toasted

1. In heavy saucepan, bring 1 cup water to a boil; stir in coffee until dissolved. Reduce heat; add marshmallows and margarine. Cook and stir over low heat until marshmallows are melted and mixture is smooth.
2. Set saucepan in ice and whisk mixture constantly until cooled. Fold in whipped cream; spoon into a 9 inch graham cracker pie crust.
3. Sprinkle with walnuts. Refrigerate for at least 4 hours before serving.

Cheese Cake Pie

2 (8 ounce) packages cream cheese
3 eggs
¾ cup, plus 4 tablespoons sugar
1 ½ teaspoons vanilla
1 (8 ounce) carton sour cream

1. In mixing bowl, combine cream cheese, eggs, ¾ cup sugar and ½ teaspoon vanilla. Beat for 5 minutes.
2. Pour into a Pam sprayed 9 inch pie pan and bake at 350 degrees for 25 minutes. Cool for 20 minutes.
3. Combine sour cream, the 4 tablespoons sugar and 1 teaspoon vanilla. Pour over cooled cake. Bake 10 minutes longer. Chill at least 4 hours. Serve with your favorite fruit topping.

Peach Mousse Pie

1 (16 ounce) package frozen peach slices, thawed
1 cup sugar
1 envelope unflavored gelatin
⅛ teaspoon ground nutmeg
¾ (8 ounce) carton Cool Whip

1. Place peaches in blender; process until smooth. Place in saucepan and bring to boiling point, stirring constantly. Stir together the sugar, gelatin and nutmeg. Stir into hot puree until sugar and gelatin are dissolved.
2. Pour gelatin-peach mixture into large mixing bowl. Place in deep freeze until mixture mounds, stirring occasionally (about 20 minutes).
3. Beat mixture at high speed about 5 minutes until mixture becomes light and frothy. Fold in Cool Whip and spoon into a 9 inch graham cracker pie crust.

Incredibly good!

Creamy Pecan Pie

1 ½ cups light corn syrup
1 (3 ounce) package vanilla instant pudding
3 eggs
⅓ stick margarine, melted
2 cups pecan halves

1. Combine first 4 ingredients stirring well; stir in pecans.
2. Pour into an unbaked deep dish pie shell. Cover pie crust edges with strips of foil to prevent excessive browning.
3. Bake at 325 degrees for 35 to 40 minutes or until center of pie is set.

Dixie Pie

24 large marshmallows
1 cup evaporated milk
1 (8 ounce) carton whipping cream, whipped
3 tablespoons bourbon
1 (9 inch) prepared chocolate pie crust

1. In saucepan on low heat, melt marshmallows in milk, stirring constantly. Do not boil. Cool in refrigerator. Fold into whipped cream while adding bourbon.
2. Pour into chocolate crust. Refrigerate at least 5 hours before serving.

Black Forest Pie

1 ½ cups whipping cream, whipped
4 (1 ounce) bars unsweetened baking chocolate
1 can sweetened condensed milk
1 teaspoon almond extract
1 can cherry pie filling, chilled

1. In saucepan, over medium low heat, melt chocolate with sweetened condensed milk, stirring well to mix. Remove from heat; stir in extract. This mixture needs to cool.
2. With mixer, whip the cream. When mixture is about room temperature, pour chocolate into whipped cream and fold gently until both are well combined.
3. Pour into a prepared and cooked 9 inch pie crust. To serve, spoon a heaping spoonful of cherry pie filling over each piece of pie.

Definitely a party dessert, but the family will insist it should be served on a regular basis.

Chess Pie

1 stick butter, softened
2 cups sugar
1 tablespoon cornstarch
4 eggs
Unbaked pie crust

1. Cream together the butter, sugar and cornstarch. Add eggs, one at a time, beating well after each one added.
2. Pour mixture in pie crust. Cover pie crust edges with strips of foil to prevent excessive browning.
3. Bake at 325 degrees for 45 minutes or until center is set.

Merry Berry Pie

1 (6 ounce) package strawberry gelatin
1 cup whole berry cranberry sauce
½ cup cranberry juice cocktail
1 (8 ounce) carton Cool Whip
1 baked 9 inch pie shell

1. Dissolve gelatin in 1 cup boiling water. Add cranberry sauce and juice. Chill until it begins to thicken.
2. Fold in Cool Whip; chill again until mixture will mound. Pour into pie shell.
3. Refrigerate several hours before serving.

Peanut Butter Pie

⅔ cup crunchy peanut butter
1 (8 ounce) package cream cheese, softened
½ cup milk
1 cup powdered sugar
1 (8 ounce) carton Cool Whip

1. With mixer, blend first four ingredients and fold in Cool Whip.
2. Pour into a graham cracker crust. Refrigerate several hour before serving.

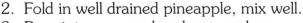
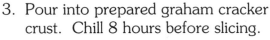

Pineapple Cheese Pie

1 (14 ounce) can sweetened condensed milk
¼ cup lemon juice
1 (8 ounce) package cream cheese, softened
1 (15 ounce) can crushed pineapple, well drained
1 (9 inch) graham cracker pie crust

1. In mixing bowl, combine condensed milk, lemon juice and cream cheese. Beat slowly at first; then beat until smooth.
2. Fold in well drained pineapple, mix well.
3. Pour into prepared graham cracker crust. Chill 8 hours before slicing.

Pineapple Lemon Pie

1 (14 ounce) can sweetened condensed milk
1 can lemon pie filling
1 (20 ounce) can crushed pineapple, well drained
1 (8 ounce) carton Cool Whip
2 cookie flavored pie crust

1. With mixer, combine condensed milk and lemon pie filling, beating until smooth.
2. Add pineapple and Cool Whip and gently fold into pie filling mixture.
3. Pour into 2 pie crusts. Refrigerate. (Eat one and freeze the other!)

Pineapple Fluff Pie

1 (20 ounce) can crushed pineapple, undrained
1 (3.4 ounce) package instant lemon pudding
1 (8 ounce) carton Cool Whip
1 (9 inch) graham cracker crust

1. In a bowl, combine the pineapple and pudding mix; beat until thickened. Fold in the Cool Whip.
2. Spoon into pie crust. Refrigerate several hours before serving.

This pie is light, airy and full of fluff. It's a perfect dessert
when you want a cool, summer finale.

Strawberry Cream Cheese Pie

2 (10 ounce) packages frozen sweetened
   strawberries, thawed
2 (8 ounce) packages cream cheese, softened
⅔ cup powdered sugar
1 (8 ounce) carton Cool Whip
1 prepared chocolate crumb crust

1. Drain strawberries, reserving ¼ cup liquid. In a mixing bowl, combine cream cheese, reserved liquid, strawberries and sugar. Beat well.
2. Fold in Cool Whip. Spoon into crust. Refrigerate overnight. Garnish with fresh strawberries.

Tumbleweed Pie

½ gallon vanilla ice cream, softened
⅓ cup plus 1 tablespoon Kahlua
⅓ cup plus 1 tablespoon Amaretto
1 (9 inch) prepared chocolate cookie crust
¼ cup slivered almonds, toasted

1. Place ice cream, Kahlua and Amaretto in mixer and blend as quickly as possible. Pour into pie crust.
2. Sprinkle almonds over top and freeze.

Yum Yum Strawberry Pie

2 pints fresh strawberries, divided
1 ¼ cups sugar
3 tablespoons cornstarch
1 (9 inch) graham cracker pie crust
1 (8 ounce) carton whipping cream, whipped

1. Crush 1 pint strawberries; add sugar, cornstarch and a dash of salt. Cook on low heat until thick and clear. Cool.
2. Place the other pint of strawberries in pie shell. Cover with cooked mixture.
3. Top with whipping cream. Refrigerate.

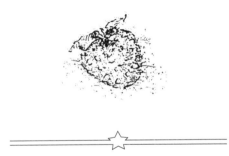

Grasshopper Pie

22 large marshmallows
⅓ cup crème de menthe
2 (8 ounce) cartons whipping cream, whipped
1 (9 inch) prepared chocolate pie crust

1. In a large saucepan, melt marshmallows with the crème de menthe over low heat.
2. Cool. Fold the whipped cream into the marshmallow mixture.
3. Pour filling into pie crust and freeze until ready to serve.

Lemonade Pie

1 (9 inch) graham cracker pie crust
½ gallon vanilla ice cream, softened
1 (6 ounce) can frozen pink lemonade, undiluted

1. With mixer, combine ice cream and frozen pink lemonade. Work quickly.
2. Pile ice cream mixture in pie crust and freeze.

Pink Lemonade Pie

1 (6 ounce) can frozen pink lemonade concentrate, thawed
1 (14 ounce) can sweetened condensed milk
1 (12 ounce) carton Cool Whip
1 graham cracker pie crust

1. In large bowl, combine lemonade concentrate and condensed milk; mixing well.
2. Fold in Cool Whip.
3. Pour into pie crust. Refrigerate several hours.

Sweet Potato Pie

1 (14 ounce) can sweet potatoes
¾ cup milk
1 cup firmly packed brown sugar
2 eggs
½ teaspoon ground cinnamon

1. Combine all ingredients plus ½ teaspoon salt, in mixer; blend until smooth.
2. Pour into a 9 inch unbaked pie crust.
3. Bake at 350 degrees for 40 minutes or until knife inserted in center comes out clean. (Shield edges of pastry with aluminum foil to prevent excessive browning.)

Easy Pumpkin Pie

1 unbaked 9 inch deep-dish pie shell
2 eggs
3 ¼ (30 ounce can) cups Libby's pumpkin pie mix
⅔ cup evaporated milk

1. Beat eggs lightly in a large bowl. Stir in pumpkin pie mix and evaporated milk. Pour into pie shell. Cut 2 inch wide strips of foil and cover pie crust edges. This will keep pie crust from getting too brown.
2. Bake at 400 degrees for 15 minutes. Reduce temperature to 350 degrees and bake for 50 more minutes or until knife inserted in center come out clean.
3. Cool.

Apricot Cobbler

1 can apricot pie filling
1 (20 ounce) can crushed pineapple, undrained
1 cup chopped pecans
1 yellow cake mix
2 sticks margarine, melted

1. Spray a 9 x 13 inch baking dish with Pam. Pour pie filling in pan and spread out.
2. Spoon pineapple and juice over pie filling. Sprinkle pecans over pineapple. Sprinkle cake mix over the pecans. Drizzle melted margarine over cake mix.
3. Bake at 375 degrees for 40 minutes or until lightly brown and crunchy. It's great topped with Cool Whip. Serve hot or room temperature.

So easy and so good!

Cherry Strawberry Cobbler

1 can strawberry pie filling
1 cans cherry pie filling
1 package white cake mix
2 sticks margarine, melted
¾ cup package slivered almonds

1. Spread pie filling in a greased 9 x 13 inch Pam sprayed baking pan. Sprinkle cake mix over the cherries.
2. Drizzle melted margarine over top. Sprinkle almonds over the top.
3. Bake at 350 degrees for 55 minutes. Top with Cool Whip.

Peach Crisp

4 ¾ cups peeled and sliced peaches
3 tablespoons lemon juice
1 cup flour
1 ¾ cups sugar
1 egg, beaten

1. Place peaches in a 9 inch baking dish and sprinkle lemon juice over top.
2. Mix together the flour, sugar, egg and a dash of salt. Spread mixture over top of peaches. Dot with a little margarine.
3. Bake at 375 degrees until golden brown.

Cherry Cinnamon Cobbler

1 can cherry pie filling
1 (12.4 ounce) tube refrigerated cinnamon rolls

1. Spread pie filling into a greased 8 inch baking dish. Set aside icing from cinnamon rolls. Arrange rolls around edge of baking dish.
2. Bake at 400 degrees for 15 minutes. Cover and bake 10 minutes longer. Spread icing over rolls. Serve warm.

Blueberry Crunch

1 (20 ounce) can crushed pineapple, undrained
1 package yellow cake mix
3 cups fresh or frozen blueberries
⅔ cup sugar
1 stick margarine, melted

1. Spread pineapple in a buttered 9 x 13 inch baking dish. Sprinkle with cake mix, blueberries and sugar. Drizzle with margarine. It is even better if you add 1 cup chopped pecans.
2. Bake at 350 degrees for 45 minutes or until bubbly.

Blueberry Cobbler

1 stick margarine, melted
1 cup self-rising flour
1 ¾ cups sugar
1 cup milk
1 can blueberry pie filling

1. Pour margarine in a 9 inch baking pan. Mix flour and sugar in a bowl. Slowly add milk and stir. Pour over melted margarine, but do not stir.
2. Spoon pie filling over batter and bake at 300 degrees for 1 hour.
3. To serve, top with Cool Whip.

Vanishing Butter Cookies

1 box butter cake mix
1 small package butterscotch instant pudding mix
1 cup oil
1 egg, beaten
1 ¼ cups chopped pecans

1. Mixing by hand (not with the mixer), stir together both dry ingredients and stir in oil.
2. Add the egg and mix thoroughly. Stir in pecans. With a teaspoon or a small cookie scoop, place cookie dough on cookie sheet about 2 inches apart.
3. Bake at 350 degrees for 8 or 9 minutes. Do not overcook.

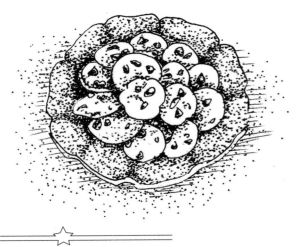

Lemon Drops

½ (8 ounce) carton Cool Whip
1 box lemon cake mix
1 egg
Powdered sugar

1. Stir, by hand, the Cool Whip into the lemon cake mix. Add egg and mix thoroughly.
2. Shape into balls. Roll in powdered sugar
3. Bake at 350 degrees for 8 to 10 minutes. Do not overcook.

Chocolate Macaroons

1 (4 ounce) package sweet baking chocolate
2 egg whites, room temperature
½ cup sugar
¼ teaspoon vanilla
1 (7 ounce) can flaked coconut

1. Place chocolate in top of a double boiler. Cook until chocolate melts, stirring occasionally. Remove from heat and cool.
2. Beat egg whites at high speed for 1 minute. Gradually add sugar, 1 tablespoon at a time, beating until stiff peaks form (about 3 minutes). Add chocolate and vanilla, beat well. Stir in coconut.
3. Drop by teaspoonfuls onto cookie sheet lined with brown paper. Bake at 350 degrees for 12 to 15 minutes. Transfer cookies, leaving them on brown paper, to cooling rack; cool. Carefully remove cookies from brown paper.

Chocolate Chip Cheese Bars

1 (18 ounce) tube refrigerated chocolate chip cookie dough
1 (8 ounce) package cream cheese, softened
½ cup sugar
1 egg

1. Cut cookie dough in half. For crust, press half of the dough onto the bottom of a greased 9 inch square baking pan or a 7 x 11 inch baking pan.
2. In a mixing bowl, beat cream cheese, sugar and egg until smooth. Spread over crust. Crumble remaining dough over top.
3. Bake at 350 degrees for 35 to 40 minutes or until a toothpick inserted near the center comes out clean. Cool on a wire rack. Cut into bars. Refrigerate leftovers.

Chocolate Crunchies

1 (20 ounce) squares of chocolate flavored candy coating
¾ cup light corn syrup
¼ stick margarine
2 teaspoons vanilla
8 cups crispy rice cereal

1. Combine chocolate, corn syrup and margarine in top of double boiler. Heat on low; cook until coating melts. Remove from heat; stir in vanilla..
2. Place cereal in a large mixing bowl; pour chocolate mixture on top and stir until well coated.
3. Quickly spoon mixture into a buttered 9 x 13 inch dish; press firmly, using the back of a spoon. Cool completely and cut into bars.

Chocolate Kisses

2 egg whites, room temperature
⅔ cup sugar
1 teaspoon vanilla
1 ¼ cups chopped pecans
1 (6 ounce) package chocolate chips

1. Preheat oven to 375 degrees. Beat egg whites until very stiff. Blend in sugar, vanilla and a dash of salt. Fold in pecans and chocolate chips.
2. Drop on shiny side of foil on a cookie sheet.
3. Put cookies in oven; TURN OVEN OFF and leave overnight. If a little sticky, leave out in air to dry.

Chocolate Drops

1 (6 ounce) package milk chocolate chips
⅔ cup chunky peanut butter
4 ¼ cups Cocoa Krispie cereal

1. In double boiler, melt chocolate chips and stir in peanut butter.
2. Stir in cereal. Press into a 9 x 9 inch pan. Cut into bars.

good

Chocolate Crunch Cookies

1 package German chocolate cake mix with pudding
1 egg, slightly beaten
1 stick margarine, melted
1 cup crisp rice cereal

1. Combine cake mix, egg and margarine. Add cereal; stir until blended. Shape dough into 1 inch balls. Place on lightly greased cookie sheet.
2. Dip a fork in flour and flatten cookies in a crisscross pattern.
3. Bake at 350 degrees for 10 to 12 minutes. Cool.

These cookies are not only incredible easy, this recipe is wonderful for the kids when they want to bake.

Chocolate Coconut Cookies

1 cup sweetened condensed milk
4 cups coconut
⅔ cup mini semi-sweet chocolate bits
1 teaspoon vanilla
½ teaspoon almond extract

1. Combine milk and coconut – mixture will be gooey. Add chocolate bits, vanilla and almond; stir until well blended.
2. Drop by teaspoonfuls onto a Pam sprayed cookie sheet. Bake at 325 degrees for 12 minutes.
3. Store in an airtight container.

Peanut Butter-Date Cookies

1 egg, beaten
⅔ cup granulated sugar
⅓ cup packed brown sugar
1 cup chunky peanut butter
½ cup chopped dates

1. Blend egg, sugars and peanut butter, mixing thoroughly. Stir in dates. Roll into one inch balls.
2. Place on ungreased cookie sheet. Using a fork, press the ball down to about ½ inch.
3. Bake at 350 degrees for about 12 minutes. Cool before storing.

Easy Peanut Butter Cookies

1 package prepared sugar cookie dough
½ cup creamy peanut butter
½ cup mini chocolate chips
½ cup peanut butter chips
½ cup chopped peanuts

1. Beat together cookie dough and peanut butter in a large bowl until blended and smooth.
2. Stir in remaining ingredients. Drop 1 heaping tablespoon of dough onto ungreased baking sheet.
3. Bake at 350 degrees for 15 minutes. Cool on wire rack.

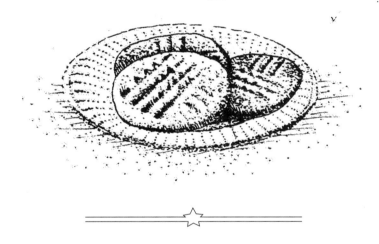

Chinese Cookies

1 (6 ounce) package butterscotch chips
1 (6 ounce) package chocolate chips
1 large can chow mein noodles
1 ¼ cups salted peanuts

1. On low heat, melt butterscotch and chocolate chips.
2. Pour over noodles and peanuts. Mix well. Drop by teaspoon onto waxed paper.
3. Refrigerate to harden. Store in airtight container.

Yummy Cookies

3 egg whites
1 ¼ cups sugar
2 teaspoons vanilla
3 ½ cups Frosted Flakes
1 cup chopped pecans

1. Beat egg whites until stiff. Gradually add sugar and vanilla.
2. Fold in Frosted Flakes and pecans. Drop by teaspoonfuls on a cookie sheet lined with waxed paper.
3. Bake at 250 degrees for 40 minutes.

Potato Chip Crispies

2 stick margarine, softened
⅔ cups sugar
1 teaspoon vanilla
1 ½ cups flour
½ cup crushed potato chips

1. Cream together the margarine, sugar and vanilla. Add flour and chips; mix well.
2. Drop by teaspoonfuls on ungreased cookie sheet.
3. Bake at 350 degrees for about 12 minutes or until lightly brown.

These are really good and crunchy!

Brown Sugar Wafers

2 sticks margarine, softened
¾ cup packed dark brown sugar
1 egg yolk
1 tablespoon vanilla
1 ¼ cups flour

1. With mixer, beat margarine, gradually adding brown sugar. Add egg yolk and vanilla, beating well.
2. Add flour and a dash of salt, mixing well. Shape dough into 1 inch balls and chill 2 hours.
3. Place on cookie sheet and flatten each cookie. Bake at 350 degrees for 10 to 12 minutes.

Angel Macaroons

1 (16 ounce) package 1-step angel food cake mix
½ cup water
1 ½ teaspoons almond extract
2 cups flaked coconut

1. With mixer, beat cake mix, water and extract on low speed for 30 seconds. Scrape bowl; beat on medium for 1 minutes. Fold in coconut.
2. Drop by rounded teaspoonfuls onto a parchment paper-lined baking sheet.
3. Bake at 350 degrees for 10 to 12 minutes or until set. Remove paper with cookies to a wire rack to cool.

Hello Dollies

1 ½ cups graham cracker crumbs
1 (6 ounce) package chocolate chips
1 cup coconut
1 ¼ cups chopped pecans
1 can sweetened condensed milk

1. Sprinkle cracker crumbs in a 9 x 9 inch pan. Layer chocolate chips, coconut and pecans. Pour condensed milk over top of layered ingredients.
2. Bake at 350 degrees for 25 to 30 minutes. Cool and cut into squares.

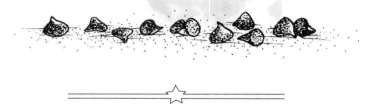

Marshmallow Treats

½ stick margarine
4 cups miniature marshmallows
½ cup chunky peanut butter
5 cups Rice Krispie cereal

1. In saucepan, melt margarine and add marshmallows. Stir until melted and add peanut butter. Remove from heat.
2. Add cereal, stirring well.
3. Press mixture into a 9 x 13 inch pan. Cut in squares when cool.

Praline Grahams

1 package graham crackers (⅓ of a 16 ounce box)
¾ cup butter
½ cup sugar
1 cup chopped pecans

1. Separate each graham cracker into four sections. Arrange in a jellyroll pan with edges touching.
2. Melt butter in a saucepan; stir in sugar and pecans. Bring to a boil; cook 3 minutes, stirring frequently.
3. Spread mixture evenly over graham crackers. Bake at 300 degrees for 10 to 12 minutes. Remove from pan and cool on wax paper. Break up to serve.

Coconut Yummies

1 (12 ounce) package white chocolate baking chips
½ stick margarine
16 large marshmallows
2 cups quick-cooking oats
1 cup flaked coconut

1. In a saucepan over low heat, melt the chocolate chips, margarine and marshmallows; stir until smooth.
2. Stir in oats and coconut; mix well.
3. Drop by rounded teaspoonfuls onto waxed paper-lined baking sheets. Chill until set. Store in air-tight container.

Sand Tarts

2 sticks butter, softened
¾ cup powdered sugar
2 cups sifted flour
1 cup chopped pecans
1 teaspoon vanilla

1. In mixer, cream together the butter and sugar; add flour, pecans and vanilla.
2. Roll into crescents and place on an ungreased cookie sheet.
3. Bake at 325 degrees for 20 minutes. Roll in extra powdered sugar after tarts have cooled.

Scotch Shortbread

1 cup butter
2 cups flour
¾ cup cornstarch
⅔ cup sugar
Granulated sugar

1. Melt butter and stir in remaining ingredients. Press into a 9 inch square pan.
2. Bake at 325 degrees for 45 minutes. Cut into squares immediately after removing from oven. Sprinkle with colored sugar sprinkles or granulated sugar.

Orange Balls

1 (12 ounce) box vanilla wafers, crushed
1 stick margarine, melted
1 (16 ounce) box powdered sugar
1 (6 ounce) can frozen orange juice, undiluted
1 cup finely chopped pecans

1. Combine wafers, margarine, sugar and orange juice, mixing well.
2. Roll into balls and roll in chopped pecans. Store in airtight container.

You can also make these in finger shapes. These make neat cookies for a party or for a tea.

Rocky Road Bars

1 (12 ounce) package semisweet chocolate morsels
1 (14 ounce) can sweetened condensed milk
2 tablespoons margarine
2 cups dry-roasted peanuts
1 (10 ounce) package miniature marshmallows

1. Place chocolate morsels, milk and margarine in top of double boiler; heat until chocolate and margarine is melted, stirring constantly.
2. Remove from heat and stir in peanuts and marshmallows.
3. Spread mixture quickly onto waxed paper-lined 9 x 13 inch pan. Chill at least 2 hours. Cut into bars and store in refrigerator.

Nutty Blonde Brownies

1 (1 pound) box light brown sugar
4 eggs
2 cups biscuit mix
2 cups chopped pecans

1. In mixer, beat together the brown sugar, eggs and biscuit mix.
2. Stir in pecans and pour into a greased 9 x 13 inch baking pan.
3. Bake at 350 degrees for 35 minutes. Cool and cut into squares.

'So easy and so very good!

Rainbow Cookie Bars

1 stick margarine
2 cups graham cracker crumbs
1 (14 ounce) can sweetened condensed milk
⅔ cup flaked coconut
1 cup chopped pecans
1 cup M & M's plain chocolate candies

1. In a 9 x 13 inch baking pan, melt margarine in oven. Sprinkle crumbs over margarine; pour condensed milk over crumbs.
2. Top with remaining ingredients; press down firmly.
3. Bake at 350 degrees for 25 to 30 minutes or until lightly browned. Cool. Cut into bars.

When making these one time, I realized I was missing the M and M's so I substituted white chocolate bits – and they were great (just not "rainbow").

Pecan Cream Cheese Squares

1 package yellow cake mix
3 eggs, divided
1 stick margarine, softened
2 cups chopped pecans
1 (8 ounce) package cream cheese, softened
3 ⅔ cups powdered sugar

1. In mixing bowl, combine cake mix, 1 egg and margarine. Stir in pecans; mix well. Press into a greased 9 x 13 inch baking pan.
2. In mixing bowl, beat cream cheese, sugar and remaining eggs until smooth. Pour over pecan mixture.
3. Bake at 350 degrees for 55 minutes or until golden brown. Cool; cut into squares.

Peanut Butter Brownies

1 (21 ounce) package brownie mix
1 cup peanut butter morsels

1. Prepare brownie mix according to package directions, stirring in peanut butter morsels. Spoon mixture into a greased 9 x 13 inch baking pan.
2. Bake at 350 degrees for 35 minutes. Cool and cut into squares.

Lemon Angel Bars

1 (1 pound) package one-step angel food cake mix
1 can lemon pie filling
⅓ cup margarine, softened
2 cups powdered sugar
2 tablespoons lemon juice

1. Combine cake mix and lemon pie filling; stir until well mixed. Pour into a greased and floured 9 x 13 inch baking pan. Bake at 350 degrees for 25 minutes.
2. Just before cake is done, mix the margarine, powdered sugar and lemon juice together and spread over hot cake.
3. When cool, cut into bars. Store in refrigerator.

Gooey Turtle Bars

1 stick margarine, melted
2 cups vanilla wafer crumbs
1 (12 ounce) semisweet chocolate morsels
1 cup pecan pieces
1 (12 ounce) jar caramel topping

1. Combine margarine and wafer crumbs in a 9 x 13 inch baking pan; press into bottom of pan. Sprinkle with chocolate morsels and pecans.
2. Remove lid from caramel topping; microwave at HIGH for ½ minute or until hot. Drizzle over pecans.
3. Bake at 350 degrees for about 10 to 15 minutes or until morsels melt; cool in pan. (Watch bars closely – you want the chips to melt, but you don't want the crumbs to burn.) Chill at least 30 minutes before cutting into squares.

Caramel Chocolate Chip Bars

1 package Caramel cake mix
2 eggs
⅓ cup firmly packed light brown sugar
½ stick margarine, softened
1 cup semi-sweet chocolate chips

1. Combine cake mix, eggs, ¼ cup water, brown sugar and margarine in large bowl. Stir until thoroughly blended. Mixture will be thick.
2. Stir in chocolate chips. Spread in a greased and floured 9 x 13 inch baking pan.
3. Bake at 350 degrees for about 25 to 30 minutes or until toothpick inserted in center comes out clean. Cool. These bars are especially good when frosted with a prepared caramel icing.

Pumpkin Cupcakes

1 (18 ounce) package spice cake mix
1 (15 ounce) can pumpkin
3 eggs
⅓ cup oil
⅓ cup water

1. With mixer, blend cake mix, pumpkin, eggs, oil and water. Beat for 2 minutes.
2. Pour batter into 24 paper-lined muffin cups. Fill ¾ full.
3. Bake at 350 degrees for 18 to 20 minutes or until toothpick inserted in center comes out clean. You might want to spread with commercial icing.

Divine Strawberries

1 quart fresh strawberries
1 (20 ounce) can pineapple chunks, well drained
2 bananas, sliced
1 (18 ounce) carton strawberry glaze

1. Cut strawberries in half or in quarters if the strawberries are very large.
2. Add pineapple chunks and bananas.
3. Fold in the strawberry glaze and chill. This is wonderful served over pound cake or just served in sherbet glasses.

This makes such a bright, pretty bowl of fruit
– besides that, it's delicious.

Coffee Surprise

1 cup strong coffee
1 (10 ounce) package large marshmallows
1 (8 ounce) package chopped dates
1 ¼ cup chopped pecans
1 (8 ounce) carton whipping cream, whipped

1. Melt marshmallows in hot coffee. Add dates and pecans. Chill.
2. When mixture begins to thicken, fold in whipped cream.
3. Pour into sherbet glasses. Place plastic wrap over top. Refrigerate.

This is a super dessert – no slicing – no "dishing up" – just
bring it right from the Frig to the table.

Kahlua Mousse

1 (12 ounce) carton Cool Whip
2 teaspoons instant coffee (dry)
5 teaspoons cocoa
5 tablespoons sugar
½ cup Kahlua liqueur

1. In large bowl, combine the Cool Whip, coffee, cocoa and sugar, blending well.
2. Fold in Kahlua.
3. Spoon into sherbet dessert glasses. Place a piece of Saran Wrap over dessert glasses until ready to serve.

Light, but rich and absolutely delicious.

Candy Store Pudding

1 cup cold milk
1 (3.4 ounce) package instant chocolate pudding mix
1 (8 ounce) carton Cool Whip
1 cup miniature marshmallows
½ cup chopped salted peanuts

1. In a bowl, whisk milk and pudding mix for 2 minutes.
2. Fold in whipped cream, marshmallows and peanuts.
3. Spoon into individual dessert dishes. Place a piece of Saran wrap over top. Refrigerate.

A special family dessert!

Cherry Trifle

1 (12 ounce) pound cake, cut into ½ inch slices
⅓ cup Amaretto
2 cans cherry pie filling
4 cups vanilla pudding
1 (8 ounce) carton Cool Whip

1. Line bottom of 3 quart trifle bowl with cake and brush with Amaretto.
2. Top with 1 cup pie filling, then 1 cup pudding. Repeat layers three times.
3. Top with Cool Whip. Chill several hours.

Caramel Amaretto Dessert

1 (9 ounce) bag small Heath bars, crumbled
30 caramels
⅓ cup Amaretto liqueur
½ cup sour cream
1 cup whipping cream

1. Reserve about ⅓ cup crumbled (not in big chunks) Heath bars. In a buttered 7 x 11 dish, spread candy crumbs.
2. In a saucepan, melt caramels with the Amaretto. Cool to room temperature.
3. Stir in creams and whip until thick. Pour into individual dessert dishes and top with reserved candy crumbs. Cover. Freeze. Cut into squares to serve

Strawberry Angel Dessert

1 (6 ounce) package strawberry gelatin
2 (10 ounce) cartons frozen strawberries,
**   undrained**
2 (8 ounce) carton whipping cream, whipped
1 large angel food cake

1. Dissolve gelatin in 1 cup boiling water; mixing well. Stir in strawberries.
2. Cool in refrigerator until mixture begins to thicken. Fold in whipped cream. Break cake into pieces and place in a 9 x 13 inch dish.
3. Pour strawberry mixture over cake. Refrigerate overnight. Cut into square to serve.

Pavlova

3 large egg whites
1 cup sugar
1 teaspoon vanilla
2 teaspoon white vinegar
3 tablespoons cornstarch

1. Beat egg whites until stiff; then add 3 tablespoons COLD water. Beat again. Add sugar very gradually white still beating. While still beating slowly, add vanilla, vinegar and cornstarch.
2. On a parchment covered cookie sheet, draw a 9 inch circle and mound the mixture within the circle.
3. Bake at 300 degrees for 45 minutes. LEAVE in oven to cool. To serve, peel paper from bottom while sliding pavlova onto a serving plate. Cover with whipped cream and top with an assortment of fresh fruit such as kiwi, strawberries, blueberries, etc.

Oreo Sunday

1 stick margarine
1 (19 ounce) package Oreos, crushed
½ gallon vanilla ice cream, softened
2 jars fudge sauce
1 (12 ounce) carton Cool Whip

1. Melt margarine in a 9 x 13 inch pan. Reserve about ½ cup crushed Oreos for top and mix remaining with margarine to form a crust in pan (press into pan).
2. Spread softened ice cream over crust (work fast); add fudge sauce on top.
3. Top with Cool Whip. Sprinkle with remaining crumbs. Freeze.

A kid's favorite!

Grasshopper Dessert

26 Oreo cookies, crushed
½ stick margarine, melted
¼ cup crème de menthe liqueur
2 (7 ounce) jars marshmallow crème
2 (8 ounce) cartons whipping cream

1. Combine cookie crumbs and margarine and press into bottom of a greased 9 inch spring form pan. Reserve about ⅓ cup crumbs for topping.
2 Gradually add crème de menthe to marshmallow crème. Whip the cream until very thick and fold into marshmallow mixture. Pour over crumbs.
3. Sprinkle remaining crumbs on top and freeze.

Ice Cream Dessert

19 ice cream sandwiches
1 (12 ounce) carton Cool Whip, thawed
1 (11 ¾ ounce) jar hot fudge ice cream topping
1 cup salted peanuts

1. Cut one ice cream sandwich in half. Place one whole and one half sandwich along a short side of an ungreased 9 x 13 inch pan. Arrange eight sandwiches in opposite direction in the pan.
2. Spread with half of the Cool Whip. Spoon fudge topping by teaspoonfuls onto Cool Whip. Sprinkle with ½ cup peanuts. Repeat layers with remaining ice cream sandwiches, Cool Whip and peanuts (pan will be full).
3. Cover and freeze. To serve, take out of freezer 20 minutes before serving.

Twinkie Dessert

1 (10 count) box Hostess Twinkies
4 bananas, sliced
1 (5.1 ounce) package vanilla instant pudding
1 (20 ounce) can crushed pineapple, drained
1 (8 ounce) carton Cool Whip

1. Slice Twinkies in half lengthwise and place in a buttered 9 x 13 inch pan, cream side up. Make a layer of sliced bananas.
2. Make pudding according to directions and pour over bananas; add the pineapple.
3. Top with Cool Whip. Refrigerate. Cut into squares to serve.

Creamy Banana Pudding

1 can sweetened condensed milk
1 (3 ¾ ounce) package instant vanilla pudding mix
1 (8 ounce) carton Cool Whip
36 vanilla wafers
3 bananas

1. In large bowl, combine condensed milk and 1 ½ cups cold water. Add pudding mix, beating well. Chill 5 minutes. Fold in Cool Whip.
2. Spoon 1 cup pudding mixture into a 3 quart glass serving bowl. Top with the wafers, bananas and pudding. Repeat layering twice, ending with pudding.
3. Cover and refrigerate.

A quick and easy way to make the old favorite banana pudding.

White Velvet

1 (8 ounce) carton whipping cream
1 ½ teaspoons unflavored gelatin
⅓ cup sugar
1 (8 ounce) carton sour cream
¾ teaspoon rum flavoring

1. Heat cream over moderate heat. Soak gelatin in ¼ cup cold water.
2. When cream is hot, stir in sugar and gelatin until dissolved. Remove from heat.
3. Fold in sour cream and flavoring. Pour into individual molds, cover with plastic wrap. Chill. Unmold to serve. Serve with fresh fruit.

Orange Cream Dessert

**2 cups crushed cream-filled chocolate cookies
(about 20)**
⅓ cup margarine, melted
1 (6 ounce) package orange gelatin
1 ½ cups boiling water
½ gallon vanilla ice cream, softened

1. In a bowl, combine cookie crumbs and margarine; set aside ¼ cup crumb mixture for topping. Press remaining crumb mixture into a greased 9 x 13 inch dish.
2. In a large bowl, dissolve gelatin in water; cover and refrigerate for 30 minutes.
3. Stir in ice cream until smooth. Work fast. Pour over the crust. Sprinkle with reserved crumb mixture. Freeze. Set out of freezer 10 or 15 minutes before serving.

Fruit Fajitas

1 can cherry pie filling (or any other pie filling)
8 large flour tortillas
1 ½ cups sugar
1 ½ sticks margarine
1 teaspoon almond flavoring

1. Divide fruit equally on tortillas, roll up and place in a 9 x 13 inch baking dish.
2. Mix together 2 cups water, sugar and margarine in saucepan and bring to a boil. Add almond flavoring and pour over flour tortillas.
3. Place in refrigerator and let soak 1 to 24 hours. Bake 350 degrees for 20 minutes or until brown and bubbly. Serve hot or room temperature.

Mango Cream

2 soft mangos
½ gallon vanilla ice cream, softened
1 (6 ounce) can frozen lemonade, thawed
1 (8 ounce) carton Cool Whip

1. Peel the mangos and cut slices around the seed; then cut into small chunks.
2. In a large bowl, mix together the ice cream, lemonade and Cool Whip. Fold in the mango chunks.
3. Quickly spoon mixture into parfait glasses or sherbets; cover with Saran wrap. Place in freezer.

Blueberry Angel Dessert

1 (8 ounce) package cream cheese, softened
1 cup powdered sugar
1 (8 ounce) carton Cool Whip, thawed
1 (14 ounce) prepared angel food cake
2 cans blueberry pie filling

1. In a large mixing bowl, beat the cream cheese and sugar, fold in Cool Whip
2. Tear cake into small 1 or 2 inch cubes. Fold into cream cheese mixture and spread evenly in a 9 x 13 inch dish; top with pie filling
3. Cover and refrigerate for at least 3 hours before cutting into squares to serve.

Brandied Fruit

2 (20 ounce) cans crushed pineapple
1 (16 ounce) can sliced peaches
2 (11 ounce) cans mandarin oranges
1 (10 ounce) jar maraschino cherries
1 cup Brandy

1. Let all fruit drain for 12 hours. For every cup of drained fruit, add ½ cup sugar. Let stand 12 hours. Add brandy and spoon into a large jar; store in refrigerator.
2. This mixture needs to stand in refrigerator for 3 weeks. Serve over ice cream.

Brandied Apples

1 loaf pound cake
1 can apple pie filling
½ teaspoon allspice
2 tablespoons brandy
Vanilla ice cream

1. Slice pound cake and place on dessert plates. In saucepan, combine pie filling, allspice and brandy. Heat and stir just until heated thoroughly.
2. Place several spoonsful over cake. Top with a scoop of vanilla ice cream.

Baked Custard

3 cups milk
3 eggs
¾ cup sugar
¼ teaspoon salt
1 teaspoon vanilla

1. Scald milk. Beat eggs, adding sugar, salt and vanilla.
2. Pour scalded milk slowly into egg mixture.
3. Pour into a 2 quart baking dish and sprinkle a little cinnamon on top. Bake, at 350 degrees in hot water bath for 45 minutes.

Individual Meringues

1(1 pound) box powdered sugar
6 egg whites, room temperature
1 teaspoon cream of tartar
½ teaspoon vanilla
1 teaspoon vinegar

1. With mixer, beat together the sugar and egg whites at high speed for 10 minutes.
2. Add cream of tartar, vanilla and vinegar and beat another 10 minutes.
3. Spoon individual meringues on greased cookie sheet. Bake at 250 degrees for 15 minutes. Then raise temperature to 300 degrees and bake another 12 minutes. Remove immediately from cookie sheet and store between sheets of waxed paper in tightly closed containers.

Cinnamon Cream

1 box cinnamon graham crackers
2 (5 ounce) packages instant French vanilla pudding mix
3 cups milk
1 (8 ounce) carton Cool Whip
1 (18 ounce) prepared caramel frosting

1. This dessert must be made the day before serving. Line bottom of a 9 x 13 inch casserole dish with graham crackers. You will be using ⅓ of the graham crackers.
2. With mixer combine vanilla pudding and milk; whip until thick and creamy. Fold in Cool Whip. Pour half pudding mixture over graham crackers. Top with another layer of graham crackers. Then add the remaining pudding mixture.
3. Top with final layer of graham crackers (you will have a few crackers left). Spread frosting over last layer of graham crackers. Refrigerate overnight.

Lime Angel Dessert

1 (6 ounce) package lime gelatin
1 (20 ounce) can crushed pineapple, undrained
1 tablespoon lime juice, 1 tablespoon sugar
1 (8 ounce) cartons whipping cream, whipped
1 large angel food cake

1. Dissolve gelatin in 1 cup boiling water; mixing well. Stir in pineapple and lime juice and sugar.
2. Cool in refrigerator until mixture begins to thicken. Fold in whipped cream. Break cake into pieces and place in a 9 x 13 inch dish.
3. Pour pineapple mixture over cake. Refrigerate overnight. Cut into squares to serve.

Baked Applesauce

5 pounds tart green apples, peeled, cored, sliced
1 (8 ounce) jar plum jelly
½ cup sugar
⅓ cup lemon juice
¼ teaspoon ground nutmeg

1. Place apples in a 2 quart casserole. In saucepan, combine jelly, sugar and ⅔ cup water. Heat until jelly is melted. Remove from heat and stir in lemon juice and nutmeg. Pour over apples.
2. Bake, covered at 350 degrees for 1 hour and 15 minutes or until apples are soft.

Delicious served with pork.

Crazy Cocoa Crisps

24 ounces white almond bark
2 ¼ cups Cocoa Krispies
2 cups dry roasted peanuts

1. Place almond bark in double boiler; heat and stir while bark is melting.
2. Stir in cereal and peanuts.
3. Drop by teaspoon on cookies sheet. Store in airtight container.

Peanut Krispies

1 stick margarine
2 cups peanut butter
1 (16 ounce) box powdered sugar
3 1/2 cups Rice Krispies
3/4 cups chopped peanuts

1. Melt margarine in a large saucepan. Add peanut butter and mix well.
2. Add powdered sugar, Rice Krispies and peanuts. Mix.
3. Drop by teaspoonsfull onto wax paper.

Scotch Crunchies

½ cup crunchy peanut butter
1 (6 ounce) package butterscotch bits
2 ½ cups Frosted Flakes
½ cup peanuts

1. Combine peanut butter and butterscotch bits in a large saucepan; melt over low heat. Stir until butterscotch bits are melted.
2. Stir in cereal and peanuts. Drop by teaspoonfuls onto wax paper.
3. Refrigerate until firm. Store in air-tight container.

White Chocolate Salties

8 (2 ounce) squares almond bark
1 cup salted Spanish peanuts
3 cups thin pretzel sticks, broken up

1. Place almond bark in top of double boiler; heat and stir until almond bark is melted. Remove from heat. Cool 2 minutes.
2. Add peanuts and pretzels; stir until coated.
3. Drop by teaspoonfuls onto wax paper. Chill 20 minutes or until firm.

Crispy Fudge Treats

6 cups crisp rice cereal
¾ cup powdered sugar
1 ¾ cups semisweet chocolate chips
½ cup light corn syrup
⅓ cup margarine

1. Combine cereal and sugar in large bowl; set aside. Place chocolate chips, corn syrup and margarine in a 1 quart microwave safe dish. Microwave, uncovered on high for about 1 minute; stir until smooth. If you have vanilla on hand, stir in 2 teaspoons vanilla.
2. Pour over cereal mixture; mix well.
3. Spoon into a greased 9 x 13 inch pan. Refrigerate for 30 minutes; cut into squares.

Tumbleweeds

1 (12 ounce) can salted peanuts
1 (7 ounce) can potato sticks, broken up
3 cups butterscotch chips
3 tablespoons peanut butter

1. Combine peanuts and potato sticks in a bowl; set aside.
2. In microwave, heat butterscotch chips and peanut butter at 70% power for 1 to 2 minutes or until melted; stir every 30 seconds. Add to peanut mixture; stir to coat evenly.
3. Drop by rounded tablespoonfuls onto waxed paper-lined baking sheet. Refrigerate until set, about 10 minutes.

Caramel Crunch

½ cup firmly packed brown sugar
½ cup light corn syrup
4 tablespoons butter (no margarine)
6 cups Chex cereal
2 cups peanuts

1. In large saucepan, heat sugar, syrup and butter. Heat until sugar and butter are melted, stirring constantly.
2. Add cereal and peanuts, stirring until all ingredients are well coated.
3. Spread mixture on a lightly greased cookie sheet and bake at 250 degrees for 30 minutes. Stir occasionally white baking. Cool. Store in airtight container.

Butterscotch Peanuts

1 (12 ounce) package butterscotch morsels
2 cups chow mein noodles
1 cup dry roasted peanuts

1. In a saucepan, heat butterscotch morsels over low heat until completely melted.
2. Add noodles and peanuts and stir until each piece is coated. Drop from spoon onto wax paper. Cool. Store in airtight container.

Peanut Clusters

1 (24 ounce) package almond bark
1 (12 ounce) package milk chocolate chips
5 cups salted peanuts

1. In double boiler, melt the almond bark and chocolate chips.
2. Stir in peanuts and drop by teaspoons onto waxed paper. Store in airtight container.

Roasted Mixed Nuts

1 pound mixed nuts
¼ cup maple syrup
2 tablespoons brown sugar
1 envelope Ranch salad dressing mix

1. In a bowl, combine nuts and maple syrup; mix well.
2. Sprinkle with brown sugar and salad dressing mix; stir gently to coat. Spread in a greased 10 x 15 inch baking pan.
3. Bake at 300 degrees for 25 minutes or until lightly browned. Cool.

Spiced Pecans

2 cups sugar
2 teaspoons cinnamon
1 teaspoon ground nutmeg
½ teaspoon ground cloves
4 cups pecan halves

1. Combine the sugar, cinnamon, nutmeg, cloves and ½ cup water and ¼ teaspoon salt. Mix well and cover with waxed paper. Microwave on high for 4 minutes. Stir.
2. Microwave another 4 minutes. Add pecans, quickly mixing well. Spread out on waxed paper to cool.
3. Break apart and store in covered container.

You can't eat just one!

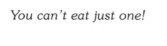

Toasted Pecans

12 cups pecan halves
1 stick margarine
Salt

1. Place pecans in a large baking pan. In 250 degree oven, toast pecans for 30 minutes to dry. Slice margarine and let pecans get completely greasy, stirring twice.
2. After pecans and margarine have mixed well, sprinkle with salt and stir often.
3. Toast pecans one hour until margarine has been absorbed and pecans are crisp.

Sugared Pecans

½ **cup packed brown sugar**
¼ **cup sugar**
½ **cup sour cream**
⅛ **teaspoon salt**
3 **cups pecan halves**

1. Combine sugars and sour cream and stir over medium heat until sugar is dissolved. Boil to soft ball stage. Add salt. Remove from heat.
2. Add pecans and stir until they are coated. Pour onto waxed paper and separate pecans carefully. They will harden after several minutes.

Honeycomb Pecans

2 **cups sugar**
2 **tablespoons honey**
2 **teaspoons vanilla**
1 **teaspoon rum flavoring**
3 **cups whole pecans**

1. Combine sugar, ½ cup water and honey in a saucepan, stirring to mix. Bring mixture to a boil (do not stir) and cook to soft ball stage (240 degrees). Remove from heat; add flavorings and cool to lukewarm. Beat with mixer 2 to 3 minutes or until mixture turns creamy.
2. Add pecans, stirring until coated. Drop by heaping tea-spoonfuls onto waxed paper.
3. Cool.

Cinnamon Pecans

1 pound shelled pecan halves
1 egg white, slightly beaten with fork
2 tablespoons cinnamon
¾ cup sugar

1. Combine the pecan halves with the egg white and mix well. Sprinkle with mixture of the cinnamon and sugar. Stir until all pecans are coated.
2. Spread on a cookie sheet and bake at 325 degrees for about 20 minutes. Cool. Store in a covered container.

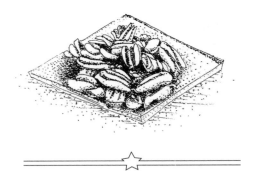

Fun to Make Sweet Pickles

1 quart whole sour pickles
3 ¼ cups sugar
1 clove garlic, finely chopped
½ teaspoon ground cloves

1. Pour off liquid from pickles; discard. Slice pickles in ¼ inch slices and place in large bowl. Add sugar, garlic and cloves. Mix and leave at room temperature until sugar is dissolved.
2. Spoon all back into jar. Seal and refrigerate. Ready to eat after 3 days.

Sweet and Sour Pickles

1 quart dill pickles, sliced (save juice)
1 ½ cups sugar
½ cup white vinegar
¾ teaspoon mustard seeds

1. Set aside juice. Place pickles in a bowl and cover with sugar. Let soak overnight.
2. Place pickles back in jar.
3. Heat juice, vinegar and mustard seeds to a boiling point and pour over pickles. Let set overnight.

Chocolate Crunchies

10 (2 ounce) squares chocolate-flavored candy coating
1 cup light corn syrup
½ stick margarine
2 teaspoon vanilla
1 (7.2 ounce) package crispy rice cereal

1. Combine chocolate candy coating, corn syrup and margarine in top of double boiler; Heat on low; cook until coating melts. Remove from heat; stir in vanilla.
2. Place cereal in a large mixing bowl; pour chocolate mixture on top and stir until well coated.
3. Quickly spoon mixture into a buttered 9 x 13 inch dish; press firmly, using the back of a spoon. Cool completely and cut into bars.

Tiger Butter

1 pound white chocolate or almond bark
½ cup chunky peanut butter
1 cup semisweet chocolate morsels

1. Line a 15 x 10 inch jellyroll pan with wax paper. Heat white chocolate in a Microwave-safe bowl on high 1 to 2 minutes or until melted. Stir until smooth.
2. Add peanut butter and microwave on high until melted. Stir again until smooth. Spread mixture evenly into prepared pan.
3. In another microwave-safe bowl melt chocolate morsels on high until melted. Pour chocolate over peanut butter mixture and swirl through with a knife until you get desired effect. Refrigerate several hours until firm. Break into pieces.

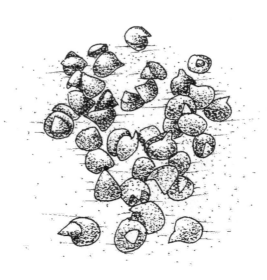

Macadamia Candy

2 (3 ounce) jars Macadamia nuts
1 (20 ounce) package of white almond bark
¾ cup coconut

1. Heat a dry skillet; toast nuts until slightly golden. (Some brands of Macadamas nuts are already toasted so skip this step if they are.) Set aside.
2. In a double boiler, melt the 12 squares of almond bark. As soon as almond bark is melted, pour the Macadamia nuts and coconut in. Stir well.
3. Place a piece of waxed paper on a cookie sheet and pour the candy on the waxed paper; spread out. Refrigerate 30 minutes to set. Break unto pieces.

When I want to make a candy that is special and one that most people have not eaten – this is the candy I make. And is it ever great!

Chocolate
Peanut Butter Drops

1 cup sugar
½ cup light corn syrup
¼ cup honey
1 (12 ounce) jar chunky peanut butter
4 cups chocolate flavored frosted corn puff cereal

1. Combine first 3 ingredients in a Dutch oven; bring to a boil, stirring constantly.
2. Remove from heat; add peanut butter, stirring until blended.
3. Stir in cereal; drop by tablespoonfuls onto wax paper. Cool.

White Chocolate Fudge

1 (8 ounce) package cream cheese, softened
4 cups powdered sugar
1 ½ teaspoons vanilla extract
12 ounces almond bark, melted
¾ cup chopped pecans

1. Beat cream cheese at medium speed with mixer until smooth; gradually add sugar and vanilla, beating well.
2. Stir in melted almond bark and pecans. Spread into a buttered 8 inch square pan. Refrigerate until firm. Cut into small squares.

This is a little different slant to fudge
— really creamy and really good!

Creamy Peanut Butter Fudge

3 cups sugar
1 ½ stick margarine
⅔ cup evaporated milk
**1 (10 ounce) package peanut butter flavored
    morsels**
1 (7 ounce) jar marshmallow crème

1. Combine first 3 ingredients in a large saucepan. Bring to a boil over medium heat, stirring constantly. Cover and cook 3 minutes without stirring. Uncover and boil 5 minutes (do not stir).
2. Remove from heat; add morsels, stirring until morsels have melted. Stir in marshmallow crème and 1 teaspoon vanilla.
3. Pour into buttered 9 x 13 inch pan. Place in freezer for 10 minutes.

Diamond Fudge

1 (6 ounce) package semisweet chocolate morsels
1 cup creamy peanut butter
1 stick margarine
1 cup powdered sugar

1. Cook first 3 ingredients in a saucepan over low heat, stirring constantly, just until mixture melts and is smooth. Remove from heat.
2. Add powdered sugar, stirring until smooth.
3. Spoon into a buttered 8 inch square pan; chill until firm. Let stand 10 minutes at room temperature before cutting into squares. Store in refrigerator.

Karo Caramels

2 cups sugar
1 ¾ cups light Karo syrup
1 stick margarine
2 (8 ounce) cartons whipping cream
1 ¼ cups chopped pecans, toasted

1. In saucepan, combine sugar, syrup, margarine and 1 cup cream. Bring to a boil. While boiling, add second cup of cream. Cook to soft ball stage.
2. Beat by hand for 3 to 4 minutes.
3. Add pecans. Pour onto a buttered platter. Cut when cool.

Microwave Fudge

3 cups semisweet chocolate morsels
1 can sweetened condensed milk
½ stick margarine, cut into pieces
1 cup chopped walnuts

1. Combine first 3 ingredients in a 2 quart glass bowl. Microwave at MEDIUM 4 to 5 minutes, stirring at 1 ½ minutes intervals.
2. Stir in walnuts and pour into a buttered 8 inch square dish. Chill 2 hours. Cut into squares.

Microwave Pralines

1 ½ cups packed brown sugar
⅔ cup half and half
Dash of salt
2 tablespoons melted margarine
1 ⅔ cups pecans, chopped

1. Combine first 3 ingredients in a deep glass dish, mixing well. Blend in margarine. Microwave on high for 10 minutes, stirring once. Stir in pecans.
2. Cool for 1 minute. Beat by hand until creamy and thickened about 4 to 5 minutes. The mixture will lose some of its gloss.
3. Drop by tablespoonful onto waxed paper.

Peanut Brittle

2 cups sugar
½ cup light corn syrup
2 cups dry-roasted peanuts
1 tablespoon margarine
1 teaspoon baking soda

1. Combine first 2 ingredients in a saucepan; cook over low heat, stirring constantly until sugar dissolves. Cover and cook over medium heat another 2 minutes.
2. Uncover, add peanuts and cook stirring occasionally to hard crack stage (300 degrees). Stir in margarine and soda. Pour into a buttered jelly roll pan, spreading thinly.
3. Let cool and break into pieces.

Peanut Butter Fudge

12 ounces chunky peanut butter
12 ounces package milk chocolate chips
1 can sweetened condensed milk
1 cup chopped pecans

1. Melt peanut butter and chocolate chips.
2. Add condensed milk and heat. Add pecans, mixing well.
3. Pour into a 9 x 9 inch buttered dish.

Sugar Plum Candy

1 ¼ pounds vanilla-flavored almond bark, cut up
1 ½ cups red and green tiny marshmallows
1 ½ cups peanut butter cereal
1 ½ cups crisp rice cereal
1 ½ cups mixed nuts

1. In a double boiler, on low heat, melt the almond bark.
2. Place marshmallows, cereals and nuts in a large bowl. Pour melted bark over the mixture, stirring to coat.
3. Drop mixture by teaspoonfuls onto waxed paper lined cookie sheet. Let stand until set. Store in airtight container.

Easy Holiday Mints

1 (16 ounce) package powdered sugar
3 tablespoons margarine, softened
3 ½ tablespoons evaporated milk
¼ to ½ teaspoon peppermint or almond extract
Few drops of desired food coloring

1. Combine all ingredients in a large mixing bowl; knead mixture in bowl until smooth.
2. Shape mints in rubber candy molds and place on baking sheets; cover with a paper towel and let dry. Store in an airtight container.

Nutty Haystacks

1 pound candy orange slices, cut up
2 cups coconut
2 cups chopped pecans
1 can sweetened condensed milk
2 cups powdered sugar

1. Place first 4 ingredients in a baking dish and cook at 350 degrees for 12 minutes, until bubbly.
2. Add powdered sugar and mix well.
3. Drop by teaspoon on waxed paper.

INDEX

COOKBOOKS PUBLISHED
BY COOKBOOK RESOURCES

Mother's Recipes

Recipe Keepsakes

Quick Fixes With Mixes

Cooking With 5 Ingredients

Kitchen Keepsakes & More Kitchen Keepsakes

Mealtimes and Memories

Best of Busy People's Cookbook Resources

Cookbook 25 Years

Texas Longhorn Cookbook

Holiday Treats

Homecoming

Cookin' With Will Rogers

Best of Lone Star Legacy Cookbook

Little Taste of Texas

Little Taste of Texas II

Southwest Sizzler

Please send_____copies of **Cooking With 5 Ingredients**

@ $ 19.95 (U.S.) each	$_____
Plus postage/handling @4.00 each	$_____
Texas residents add sales tax @ $1.30 each	$_____
Check or Credit Card (Canada-credit card only) Total	$_____

Charge to my ❑ MasterCard. or ❑ VISA

Account # _____

Expiration Date _____

Signature _____

Mail or Call:
Cookbook Resources
541 Doubletree Drive
Highland Village, TX 75077
(972) 317-0245
sheryn@cookbookresources.com

Name _____

Address _____

City _____ State _____ Zip _____

Phone (day) _____ (night) _____

— —

Please send_____copies of **Cooking With 5 Ingredients**

@ $ 19.95 (U.S.) each	$_____
Plus postage/handling @4.00 each	$_____
Texas residents add sales tax @ $1.30 each	$_____
Check or Credit Card (Canada-credit card only) Total	$_____

Charge to my ❑ MasterCard. or ❑ VISA

Account # _____

Expiration Date _____

Signature _____

Mail or Call:
Cookbook Resources
541 Doubletree Drive
Highland Village, TX 75077
(972) 317-0245
sheryn@cookbookresources.com

Name _____

Address _____

City _____ State _____ Zip _____

Phone (day) _____ (night) _____